THE
MADISON
REGATTA

THE MADISON REGATTA

Hydroplane Racing in Small-Town Indiana

FRED FARLEY & RON HARSIN

Charleston · London

THE
History
PRESS

Published by The History Press
Charleston, SC 29403
www.historypress.net

First published 2011

Manufactured in the United States

ISBN 978.1.60949.300.4

Library of Congress Cataloging-in-Publication Data
Farley, Fred.
The Madison Regatta : hydroplane racing in small-town Indiana / Fred Farley and Ron
Harsin.
p. cm.
ISBN 978-1-60949-300-4
1. Motorboat racing--Indiana--Madison--History. 2. Hydroplanes--Indiana--Madison--
History. 3. Regattas--Indiana--Madison--History. I. Harsin, Ron. II. Title.
GV835.9.F38 2011
797.1'40977213--dc22
2011012306

This book is dedicated to one of hydroplane racing's most respected veterans:

Mr. Graham Heath

formerly of Madison, Indiana.

The above photo shows the authors of this book with Graham Heath and his wife.
Left to right: Fred Farley, Hazel Heath, Graham Heath and Ron Harsin

CONTENTS

CONTENTS

MY "WALK-ON PART" IN THE MADISON LEGACY

The town and team this book is about are as fundamentally American as mom and apple pie. Born as a frontier town, maturing into a major river port on the Ohio River, home to industry from the 1800s to this very day and facing struggles of every sort, it survives. These Hoosiers are a hearty bunch, and I have a front-row seat to their story. For the first thirteen years of my Unlimited hydroplane driving career, they, amongst others, were my competition.

I stepped away from the sport midway through the 1999 season after my father died. Dad had been my racing partner since birth, and without him with me, it became void of passion. Enter my adopted town of Madison. Charlie Grooms, team manager of the *Miss Madison* Unlimited hydroplane, called me in February 2001. In the straightforward, look-you-in-the-eye way of midwesterners, and Madisonians in particular, he asked, "Are you done with your pity party and ready to race again?" Thus began my "walk-on part."

While that was Charlie speaking, I know it was Dad in heaven who wrote the script. You see, the *Madison*, their boat, had always been his favorite. Imagine my dad rooting for my competition! Now, almost eleven years later, I know why he loved them. He knew, as I do now, that when the right ingredients come together in a race program, magic happens.

It isn't just one person or bountiful funding that makes a winner. It is the input of lots of people from varying backgrounds, with a common purpose and a deep passion. This passion, this drive, fueled the birth of the town

of Madison and, to this day, fuels the number one Unlimited hydroplane in the world.

In truth, I'm just a visitor to this team, its driver for coming on eleven seasons now. But I also know that I'm a part of its legacy. A part that I can never forget didn't start with me and will not end with me, yet a part that is as much a part of me as my heart and lungs. These people are my family; this boat is in my blood. When I drive the *Miss Madison* (sponsored and known in racing circles as the Oh Boy! Oberto, the souls of every Madisonian who has backed this team for the past fifty-plus years rides with me. They've been racing longer than any race team in any motor sport in history. I know that our racing can bring cheers or tears, based largely on what I do. This is no small responsibility. Nor is it any small honor.

As you read through these pages, lovingly crafted by two of the best writers in motor sports, I hope you feel the same passion for this town and this boat as I do. Better yet, drop by Madison any July Fourth weekend to witness its regatta. For sixty years, they've staged the largest motor sport event in Indiana, outside of the Indianapolis 500. As you walk the streets of Madison, you will undoubtedly feel the energy that is embedded in its brick streets, its vintage homes and its people. You'll sense what it is that gives America heart and what continues to fuel this town and this team.

Live well,
Steve David
National Driving Champion 2005, 2006, 2008, 2009, 2010

ACKNOWLEDGEMENTS

The authors are indebted to all who helped make this book a reality.
A special thanks in the memory of Ms. Rita Cline for providing her collection of past Madison Regatta programs for use in collecting information and photos for this book.

Thanks to David and Jean Johnson for opening their hydroplane museum to the authors and for giving their time and assistance in the creation of this book.

We wish to thank Joseph and Janice Johnson for their ongoing assistance.

We also wish to thank Tom and Jacqueline Bertolini for allowing us access to the boats, drivers and crew members at the race sites; without this access, a majority of the information in this book would have never become available.

Special thanks to everyone who allowed us to use their photos and art designs, especially the *Madison Courier*, *RoundAbout Madison*, *Propeller Magazine*, *Today's Sports Magazine*, *SkidFin Magazine*, and the *Unlimited News Journal*.

We wish to thank all of the photographers who contributed photos to this book, including the Madison Historic Society, Rita and Robert Cline, David and Jean Johnson, Dale Wilson, Mark Campbell, Don Ward, David Williams, Bob Carver, Rich Ormbrek, Ron Harsin, Carl Trivett, Thayer Cueter, Russell Bishop, Mark Terao, Clifford Ellis, Brad Luce, Bill Osborne, Phil Kunz, P. Gleeson, Hal Stein, Ray Krantz, John C. Hillery, Bill DeGlopper, Bill and Judy Fisk, Leslie Field, the Towne Studio, Brian Reed, Unlimiteds Detroit, Jeff Dunn, Mike Millenbach, Vicki Fewell, Bill Knodell, Randy Roe, Bernie Schwartz, Larry Wilson, Denise Taylor, Tom Turrill,

Acknowledgements

James Mead, Jim Smith, Tom Harvey, Bill Grunow, Mike McCormick, C. Looney, Chip Dogwill, Dave Mabry, Denny Jackson, Don Gold, Duane Hover, Gerry Sieracki, Hank Kosciuszko, Roger Schaaf, Scott Dunn, Terri Garey, Ed Krupinski, David Ruiga, Ron Grimes and Joe Carr.

Many of the photographs in this book are reproduced from historical archives, and therefore, the quality varies widely throughout. We have reproduced all the photographs using the latest techniques in order to match the original photographs as closely as possible.

Thank you to our families for enduring all the hours while we worked on this book.

To the many people who helped in so many ways—their names are too numerous to mention, but to all of you—THANK YOU!!

IN THE BEGINNING

Madison, Indiana, may rank as the smallest town on the H1 Unlimited hydroplane tour in terms of population (thirteen thousand), but the picturesque Ohio River Valley community stands head and shoulders above many a larger metropolis with its rich powerboat racing heritage.

Every Fourth of July weekend, the town hosts the latest in a long line of nationally prominent motor sport spectaculars to be presented on the historic Ohio River racecourse.

The current series of Madison Regattas began in 1949. But the tradition began long before that.

***

Think back to an earlier—and simpler—time, in the days prior to the American Civil War. Numerous accounts can be found of the huge paddlewheelers and sternwheelers that plied their trade on the legendary Ohio River. The first steamship to navigate the river in the vicinity of Madison was the *New Orleans* in 1811. Commander Nicholas Roosevelt commanded this famous ship. He was the great-grandfather of future first lady of the United States Anna Eleanor Roosevelt.

By 1829, the commerce generated by steamboat traffic was instrumental in establishing Madison as a vital trade center in the Midwest. The Ohio

Steamship *New Orleans*.

River steamers brought sugar, rice, cotton, coffee, molasses and other commodities from the South to Madison to be distributed through Indiana and into Michigan, while Indiana farm products were brought to town and set aboard the river freighters to be transported to other points of trade.

The competitive spirit of the captains of the nineteenth-century riverboats remains engrained in the culture of the Ohio River Valley. Perhaps this is why local folks take boat racing far more seriously than do persons in other parts of the country.

In the words of Madison author and historian David L. Taylor, "Stories have been handed down through the years of not only races between riverboats, in head-to-head competition, but of boat captains attempting to better the quickest time between ports. These frequent and celebrated competitions were more than just races. The victor often found himself blessed with a ready freight, a full load, and therefore, larger profits."

According to Taylor, "In the 1820s, the passing of a steamboat was a grand occasion in Madison with the whole town turning out to watch."

The *Madison Daily Tribune* reported in 1851, "The time of the [steamboat] Telegraph from Louisville to the wharf at Madison was three hours and thirty-nine minutes, the quickest time ever made."

The development of the internal combustion engine in the late 1800s signaled a new era of speed on the water—both locally and around the world. Gasoline engine–powered boats of one sort or another have been in evidence since as early as 1887, when Gottleib Daimler hitched a crude petrol motor to the rear of a rowboat, which putt-putted a few miles per hour on the river Seine in Paris.

The first successful motorboat race of the twentieth century took place on the Seine at the Paris Universal Exhibition of 1900. Eight launches competed over a 7.5-mile (12-kilometer) course. Marius Dubonnet's *L'Aiglon* ("Eaglet") was first over the finish line with a time of forty-seven minutes and fifteen seconds.

Other noteworthy races occurred at the Nice Regatta in France in 1901 and at Arcachon Bay, France, in 1902, but the world's first formal powerboat race of major importance occurred at Queenstown, Ireland, in 1903. This was for the British International ("Harmsworth") Trophy.

The 1903 Harmsworth race was won by England's *Napier I* and driven by a woman, Miss Dorothy Levitt. The narrow thirty-five-foot craft, powered by a seventy-five-horsepower Napier engine, defeated *Trefle-a-Quatre*, a French vessel, at a speed of 19.530 land miles per hour.

The first contest for the APBA Gold Cup (officially known as the American Power Boat Association Challenge Cup) was run on the Hudson River in New York in 1904 as America's answer to the highly touted Harmsworth Trophy. The Gold Cup remains in competition to this day and has been contested on the Ohio River at Madison on three occasions—in 1971, 1979 and 1980.

The 1904 Gold Cup course was 16 nautical miles up and down the Hudson, unlike the oval-shaped 2.5-mile closed course that is in use today. Carl Riotte at the helm of *Standard* won all three heats of history's first Gold Cup

The Gold Cup.

race, with a 96-mile average speed of 23.160 land miles per hour. Standard was a displacement craft, measuring 59 feet in length with an 8.5-foot beam and powered by a 110-horsepower Standard motor, which resembled a miniature steam engine with its steel columns and open frame.

During the first decade of the twentieth century, organized powerboat racing in North America was largely confined to the northeast quadrant of the United States. During the first eleven years of the APBA Gold Cup's existence, not once was it run outside of the state of New York, the cradle of powerboat competition in the United States. All of that changed when *Miss Detroit*, a single-step hydroplane equipped with a 250-horsepower Sterling engine, put in an appearance at the 1915 renewal on Manhasset Bay. Co-drivers John Milot and Jack Beebe emerged victorious with a three-heat average of 37.656 around the five-mile triangular course.

Thus, the sponsoring Miss Detroit Power Boat Association won the right to host the 1916 Gold Cup Regatta in the Motor City on the Detroit River. This introduced major league powerboat racing to the American Midwest.

Although largely unnoticed by the national powerboat community as a whole, the city of Madison in southern Indiana had a head start of several years on some of its big-city counterparts. Unclear early records contradict themselves, but informal motorboat racing occurred in Madison as early as 1910 or 1911. Most sources tend to favor 1911 as the starting point. This was around the time of the first Indianapolis 500 automobile race. The War Between the States was within the memory of many Americans still living. And World War I—the "War to End All Wars"—was still a few years in the future.

William Howard Taft was president of the United States in 1911. George V was King of England. Wilhelm II occupied the throne of Germany. The Panama Canal was still being dug. And a Maxwell touring car, four-cylinder, thirty-horsepower, of the five-bearing crankshaft variety, sold for $1,750.

That first Madison Regatta escaped notice in the *Madison Courier*, the local daily newspaper. Anecdotal evidence, however, suggests that the steamship *Princess* from Coney Island tied up in the middle of the Ohio River. Unidentified power launches ran an oval track roughly around the boat. This was one of the earliest examples of competition around a closed course, rather than the old-fashioned "bang-and-go-back" variety that characterized earlier aquatic spectacles.

The racing craft of that early era featured narrow displacement hulls that plowed through—rather than skim over—the water at around twenty miles per hour. They were a far cry from their modern counterparts that have

The *Princess* at the first known Madison Regatta.

only a nodding acquaintance with the water and throw roostertails of spray a football field in length at speeds approaching two hundred miles per hour.

Boat racers of the first decade of the twentieth century used largely vee-bottom pleasure craft, motorized fishing boats and other early motorboats. These were men unversed in racing technique but who established a pattern that—one hundred years later—is still being followed by experts.

In researching the documented history of boat racing in Madison, a number of "first annual" Madison Regattas have been identified in the years 1914, 1929, 1934 and 1949, according to the *Madison Courier*. This has caused confusion among some regatta history buffs. Be that as it may, the first regatta to be written up in the *Courier* was the 1914 event, which was described as "a big aquatic meet and water carnival," contested on September 20 of that year. A five-mile triangular course was used, with the starting line located at the foot of Poplar Street. The main event of the 1914 Madison Regatta was a free-for-all race for pleasure boats capable of speeds better than fifteen miles per hour. The reported winner was the *E.L.A.*, owned and driven by C.S. Gilbert of Jeffersonville, Indiana.

The earliest hydroplane hulls in North America were developed around 1910. At high speeds, they rode on one or more breaks or "steps" affixed to the underside, thereby using much less wetted surface area than had been the case with the old-style, vee-bottom displacement craft. These were the first boats to be designed specifically for racing. One of these, the *Dayton Kid*, owned by Pat Parrish of Dayton, Kentucky, made an exhibition appearance at the 1914 Madison Regatta.

According to the *Madison Courier*, the *Dayton Kid*'s performance "was the most spectacular run ever made by a boat on this part of the Ohio River and the crowd was astonished at the wonderful speed developed by this craft. The boat was showing from 35 to 40 miles an hour and it looked like it was traveling sixty."

In 1915, a hydroplane named *Vivo*, owned by James Howard, made a shambles of the opposition in the feature event at the Madison Regatta. Boats like *Dayton Kid* and *Vivo* clearly foreshadowed the Unlimited hydroplanes of the modern era. They were state-of-the-art for their day.

Informal racing at Madison continued for a number of years. In 1916, a "bang-and-go-back" race drew a lot of attention. Eleven boats lined up evenly at the start. A bomb exploded in the air, and the boats charged toward a buoy located a mile downstream. When the first boat reached the marker, another bomb signaled for the boats to reverse course. *Mohawk Kid*, owned by R.B. Hadley of Louisville, was the first boat back to the starting line and was declared the winner.

The *Madison Courier* described the *Mohawk Kid* as a "dumpy little 14-footer, equipped with a five-horsepower engine." The reported speed of the boat was about fifteen miles per hour.

The racing world as a whole took little notice of tiny Madison during the first quarter of the twentieth century. All of that changed in 1929, when the town hosted the first event to be sanctioned by a major powerboat organization.

Main Street, Madison, Indiana, 1909.

18

BETWEEN THE
WORLD WARS

The first major regatta to be run at Madison occurred in 1929 under the auspices of the Ohio Valley Motor Boat Racing Association (OVMBRA), which was a member club of the Mississippi Valley Power Boat Association (MVPBA). The MVPBA was the southern and midwestern counterpart of the American Power Boat Association (APBA).

The 1929 race took place just a few weeks prior to the Wall Street stock market crash, which plunged the United States into the Great Depression of the 1930s. This was also the year that saw the completion of the Milton-Madison Bridge over the Ohio River. For more than eight decades, race boats have run under the bridge, which intersects the Madison Regatta racecourse.

L.J. Montifer's *Catherine III* from Cincinnati emerged as the champion that Labor Day weekend in 1929. Equipped with a World War I vintage Hispano-Suiza ("Hisso") airplane engine, the craft won $400 for its victories in the 725 Cubic Inch Class event and both heats of the Hydroplane Free-for-All around the approximate 2.5-mile course.

The 725s were a mainstay on the MVPBA circuit during the years between the world wars. There was a considerable fleet of them around the Cincinnati and Louisville area. As the MVPBA counterpart of the APBA Gold Cup Class and the European UIM 12-Litre Class, the 725s were sometimes called the Haywire Class. They were in no sense Gold Cup boats

The 1929 Madison Regatta
Program Guide.

as boats of that class were generally thought of being. Their 719-cubic-inch "Hisso" engines, under favorable conditions, developed slightly over two hundred horsepower. The boats cost about $1,500 to $2,000 to build and make race ready.

Although a popular regional class, the 725s seldom enjoyed the level of media attention as the generally more expensive and more exotic-looking Gold Cup Class boats. The 725 Class, nevertheless, served as a calling card for some of the more popular personalities in the history of racing. These included the likes of "Wild Bill" Cantrell, Marion Cooper and George Davis, from whom much would be heard in the years ahead.

After World War II, the 725 Class and the Gold Cup Class combined and changed over to the Unlimited Class, the Thunderboats of the racing world.

Pal II, another "Hisso"-powered 725, took second to *Catherine III* in both contests in 1929 and claimed $200 for owner Russell Dowers.

Among the highlights of the 1929 Madison Regatta was an exhibition run by J.W. Whitlock's *Hoosier Boy* from Rising Sun, Indiana. The step hydroplane with the Liberty engine ran for five miles and averaged a fraction over fifty-six miles per hour for the two laps.

Hydroplane Racing in Small-Town Indiana

In those early days, boat owners often piloted their hydroplanes to the race sites by river rather than haul them by trailer over land, as was the case with *Hoosier Boy* in 1929. Owner Whitlock drove his craft down from Rising Sun, made his exhibition run and returned home after the event.

Almost five years earlier, in 1924, Whitlock had set a never-to-be-equaled distance record with an earlier *Hoosier Boy*. He drove from Cincinnati to Louisville and back to Cincinnati—a distance of 267 Ohio River miles—in 267 minutes and 49 seconds. This was just a shade less than 60 miles per hour. It is speculated that *Hoosier Boy* might have cleared 60 had it not encountered the battering wakes of a half-dozen towboats and barges along the way. All of this took place prior to construction of a series of locks and dams in the late 1920s that would make such a run impossible today.

One of racing's most famous participants made his Madison Regatta debut in 1929. This was Bill Cantrell, a native of West Point, Kentucky. Cantrell entered the Class C Outboard category with *Falls City Baby*. He flipped upside-down during a warm-up run and had to withdraw from further activity.

The front page of the *Madison Courier* proclaimed that "Madison's first Motorboat regatta will go down in history as one of the most successful events sponsored here in many years. Financially, it was self-supporting and as a means of entertainment it is unsurpassed."

Madison, Indiana, was hit hard by the Great Depression. In the words of one local resident, "There was no money, no work, and no hope." But despite the economic instability of the times, Madison remained a boat racing-oriented community and hosted many regattas in conjunction with the Mississippi Valley Power Boat Association. The city pulled off a major coup in 1930 when the MVPBA sanctioned the twenty-third annual running of its premier event—the Webb Trophy—and awarded it to Madison. The Webb Trophy, in those days, rivaled the prestigious Gold Cup award of the American Power Boat Association.

In the 1930 race, Cam Fischer in *Miss Cincinnati* tied Whitlock's *Hoosier Boy* on total points but won first prize on the basis of having turned the fastest fifteen-mile heat at 60.173 miles per hour. Other entries that year included *Louisville Kid*, *Lady Marion*, *Miss Fern Creek*, *Rascal*, *Who Cares* and *Miss Quincy XI*.

During the regatta years of 1932, 1934, 1935 and 1936, the 725 Cubic Inch Class competitors were the crowd pleasers. V.L. Bundschu won the 725 Class event in 1932 at the wheel of *Betty*, followed by *Louisville Kid* and *Who Cares*. "Soupy" Ciconette won the inboard free-for-all in 1932 with *Who Cares*.

The 1936 regatta featured a hometown entry in the person of Alvin Holsclaw, who entered his boat *Amrad* in twelve heats and finished all of them. He placed fourth in the 725 Class, first in the 510 Class and third in the 225 Class. Holsclaw built the *Amrad* himself. His total prize money for the weekend was eighty dollars.

A rather unique accident marred the running of the 1936 regatta. The Ohio River was quite rough that day. The 725 Class *Miss Cincinnati* took a bad bounce. Driver Lou Schaefer and riding mechanic J.R. Lippman were thrown into the water. The driverless craft then slammed into a Louisville-based Coast Guard patrol boat. Thankfully, there were no reported injuries. The mishap was reminiscent of a similar crash twenty-two years in the future when an out-of-control *Miss Thriftway*, driven by Bill Muncey, encountered— and sank—a Coast Guard craft during the 1958 APBA Gold Cup race on Seattle's Lake Washington.

The reigning superstar of 1930s Madison racing was clearly Bill Cantrell, who took top honors three years running—in 1934 and 1935 with Ralph Longworth's *Big Shot* and in 1936 with his self-owned *Why Worry*. This was the first in a long line of *Why Worry* hydroplanes that Cantrell was to campaign between 1936 and 1951.

The original *Why Worry* was a Hisso-powered single-step hydroplane, capable of straightaway speeds of up to sixty-one miles per hour. In addition to winning at Madison in 1936, the craft took first place in the Calvert Trophy at Louisville in 1937 and finished third in the 725 Class races at Detroit in 1937 and 1938.

The 725 Class racers often operated more on the cutting edge of boat racing technology than did their Gold Cup Class counterparts. The 725 Class teams were among the first to recognize the potential of the new-fangled three-point hydroplane design. For 1939, Cantrell unveiled a three-point *Why Worry*, Marion Cooper built *Mercury* and George Davis debuted *Hermes IV* (the future *It's a Wonder*). All three rode on the tips of two sponsons and a submerged propeller. And all three teams enjoyed successful careers on the Ohio River Valley hydroplane circuit.

About the only part of Cantrell's boat that wasn't homebuilt was the bare hull itself, which was a product of the famed Ventnor Boat Works of Ventnor, New Jersey. In certain places, baling wire was used in the 1939 *Why Worry*. The gears dated back to 1925, and a second-hand automobile wheel with wire cable constituted the steering mechanism. As the story goes, the V-8 Hispano-Suiza engine cost Cantrell $175.00. When he discovered that the type of pistons that he needed would cost $700.00, he did the work himself at a cost of $3.50 per piston.

Unfortunately, Madison Regatta fans missed the opportunity to observe in person this first generation of three-point racers. The disastrous Ohio River flood of 1937 and the advent of World War II brought down the curtain on racing at Madison for many years to come. Racing did not resume until 1949.

Stories were handed down through the years of race boats that assisted in disaster relief efforts during the 1937 flood. George Davis of Vine Grove, Kentucky, fired up the 510 Cubic Inch Class *Hermes*, powered by a Curtiss OX-5, and proceeded to the rescue of Louisville residents trapped on the roofs of their homes.

THE AMATEUR HEYDAY

With the advent of World War II and gasoline rationing, competition in virtually all classes of powerboating the world over was suspended. When racing resumed in 1946, a rejuvenated format was in evidence.

The 732-cubic-inch piston limitation was abandoned for the combined Gold Cup and 725 Cubic Inch Classes. This was necessary because there were no suitable engines being manufactured in the sizes prescribed by the then-current rules. The introduction of converted Allison and Rolls-Royce Merlin aircraft engines, developed for the war effort, produced new enthusiasm for what was now the Unlimited Class, America's premier powerboat racing category.

Competition quickly resumed in places like Detroit, Washington, D.C., and Red Bank, New Jersey, in 1946. Madison, Indiana, hosted its first postwar racing event in 1949, under the auspices of the newly organized Madison Boat Club, which later came to be known as Madison Regatta, Inc.

One of the primary movers in the revival of interest in Madison boat racing was local businessman Birl Hill. Hill had been actively involved as a boat builder and competitor in the 1930s series of Madison Regattas. His influence was keenly felt—and appreciated—from 1949 to 1959.

The 1949 Madison Regatta was a rather informal affair, conducted on October 2 of that year. But this began the string of consecutive annual races that continues uninterrupted to this day. The big winner at Madison in 1949 was Louisville resident Marion Cooper in his 225 Cubic Inch Class *Hornet*. The 225s were the largest class participating that year. Also on the program were several smaller classes of Limited Inboards and Outboards.

Twelve years later, Cooper would achieve fame as the original driver of the community-owned *Miss Madison* Unlimited hydroplane.

Another competitor in 1949 was future Unlimited Class luminary Ron Musson of Akron, Ohio. Musson did not have one of his better days at Madison that year when he flipped upside-down driving *Dauntless VII* in one of the Outboard races. But Musson was to return ten years later to win the feature Unlimited event at Madison with the famed "Pink Lady" *Hawaii Kai III*.

The 1950 regatta was the first to be sanctioned by the American Power Boat Association. It was also the first to be patronized by a modern Unlimited hydroplane. This was the *My Darling*, a step hydro from Springfield, Illinois. Powered by a twelve-cylinder Allison engine and driven by its owner, Andy Marcy, *My Darling* won the 10-mile free-for-all heat on a 2.5-mile course at about seventy-six miles per hour.

Marcy defeated Phil Rothenbusch in the 225 Class *Wild Goose* and J.D. Smith in the unnamed 48 Class Y-39. Thom Cooper, driving the 225 Class *Tops VII*, led until a piece of driftwood lodged itself in the water intake.

Oliver Elam brought a pair of boats—the 7-Litre *Mercury* and the Gold Cup Class *Ollie's Folly*—to Madison's APBA debut. He withdrew the latter and didn't finish in *Mercury*.

The APBA referee at Madison in 1950 was Jim Noonan of Louisville. Decades later, Noonan's sons Mike and Billy would follow in their father's footsteps as the Madison Regatta referees.

Phil Cole Jr., the sports editor of the *Madison Courier*, attended the 1950 Madison Regatta as a spectator. The man who was scheduled to announce the race didn't show up, so Phil was asked to pinch-hit. He did, and that was the start of a new career for Cole. For the next quarter century, the name Phil Cole became synonymous with "The Voice of Unlimited Racing." He was to boat racing what Sid Collins was to the Indianapolis 500. In the years ahead, Cole played a major role in the development of the Madison Regatta and in the establishment of the *Miss Madison* team in 1961.

The Indiana Governor's Cup tradition began in 1951. In each of the ensuing sixty years, the cup has been awarded to the winner of the feature race at the Madison Regatta. As originally envisioned, the Governor's Cup was intended as a one-heat/fifteen-mile event for classes 7 Litre and above. Two boats of that description appeared in 1951: the Unlimited Class *Gale* II, driven by Lee Schoenith, and the 725 Cubic Inch Class *It's a Wonder*, handled by George Davis. Due to the sparseness of the field, "step-ups" were invited from the smaller classes by the race committee, in accordance with APBA rules.

Marion Cooper duplicated his 1949 Madison triumph with a victory in the 1951 Indiana Governor's Cup at 65.886 miles per hour with his 225 Class *Hornet*. Don Campbell of Cincinnati was declared the second-place finisher with his 225 Class *Miss Delhi Hills*, while the third-place trophy went to Davis and *It's a Wonder*. Schoenith and *Gale II* failed to finish.

Both the 1952 and 1953 contests for the Indiana Governor's Cup were dominated by a 7-Litre Class hydroplane—the *Wildcatter*, owned and driven by the father and son team of Burnett Bartley Sr. and Jr., from Pittsburgh. Oliver Elam and the 7-Litre Class *Mercury* ran second to Bartley Jr. in 1952, while Ralph Manning and the Gold Cup Class *Ollie's Folly* finished runner-up in 1953. Claiming the third-place trophy on both occasions was *It's a Wonder* with owner-driver George Davis twice duplicating his 1951 performance in the Hisso-powered prewar contender from Vine Grove, Kentucky.

As the first two-time consecutive winner in Governor's Cup history, *Wildcatter* posted average speeds of 70.866 and 71.599 for the fifteen-mile distance.

Local sports editor Phil Cole worked tirelessly on behalf of the Madison Regatta in the 1950s under race Chairman Birl Hill. Up until 1953, all of the Unlimited races run at Madison consisted of only one heat and were really just free-for-alls for classes 7 Litre and above. Never more than one or two Unlimiteds ever showed up. Nothing counted for APBA National High Points.

Cole was anxious to see Madison advance to the next level with a full-fledged Unlimited race with High Points at stake. For that to happen, a race had to be scheduled for a minimum of two heats with at least four boats making a legal start.

That was easier said than done. In the 1950s, there was no Unlimited circuit per se, because the sport was very regional. About the only time that all of the top Unlimiteds were ever in the same pit area was at the Gold Cup.

The "big-city" races, such as Seattle, Detroit or Washington, D.C., were generally well attended. But it was pretty much catch as catch can where the smaller communities were concerned. Lots of these had trouble attracting boats during the 1950s. (These included Elizabeth City, North Carolina; New Martinsville, West Virginia; and Polson, Montana.) According to Cole, "All we in Madison could do was try to make friends with the owners and try to persuade them to enter our race."

Phil was determined that Madison, Indiana, would not "die on the vine" as so many other race sites had. By hook or by crook, he was going to recruit a representative field of Unlimiteds for a race that counted for National High Points. And he succeeded! How he went about this was quintessential Phil Cole.

As race day neared for the 1954 Madison Regatta, two teams—the *Miss Cadillac* and the *Dora My Sweetie*, both from Detroit—signified their intentions to attend. But the crews let it be known that they were coming to town primarily for a fun weekend and to put on an exhibition. They didn't want to have to go all out and really race anybody.

Cole and his friend Bill Cantrell cooked up a scheme. Cantrell agreed to bring the nationally ranked team of *Gale IV* and *Gale V*, which he and Lee Schoenith drove, to Madison. But it was important that the *Miss Cadillac* and *Dora My Sweetie* teams not know about it. So Cantrell stored the two *Gale*s at Soupy Ciconett's boat shop in Louisville for a few days. Only at the last moment did the *IV* and the *V* pull into the pits at Madison.

Seeing the *Gale IV* and the *Gale V* arrive on the scene almost sent *Miss Cadillac* owner Frank "Bud" Saile into cardiac arrest. ("If I had known they were going to be here, I wouldn't have come!") But now it was too late for *Miss Cadillac* and *Dora My Sweetie* to gracefully withdraw. They had to put on a real race.

That's how Madison, Indiana, hosted its first-ever National High Points event, which was won by "co-conspirator" Cantrell in *Gale IV*. Madison has staged a High Points race for Unlimited hydroplanes every year since. (Only Detroit and Seattle have hosted more Points races than Madison.)

Beginning in 1954, the Madison Regatta's main event became an exclusive Unlimited affair. This was also the first year in which a multi-heat format was used for the Indiana Governor's Cup.

Owned by Joe Schoenith, the Allison-powered *Gale IV* from Detroit won the final heat at 91.556, in spite of a large hole in the port sponson, followed by Jack Bartlow in *Dora My Sweetie*, Lee Schoenith in *Gale V* and Saile in *Miss Cadillac*.

Bill Cantrell's 1954 victory was his fourth in Madison as a driver. Previously, in the 725 Class era, Bill had won the top prize with *Big Shot* in 1934 and 1935 and with *Why Worry* in 1936. Following his retirement from competition, Cantrell entered the Madison winners' circle twice more as team manager in 1969 with *MYR's Special* and driver Dean Chenoweth and in 1972 with *Atlas Van Lines* and driver Bill Muncey.

The first heat to be timed at over 100 miles per hour in Ohio River history was recorded in heat one of the 1955 Indiana Governor's Cup. Danny Foster averaged 102.079 for the fifteen-mile distance with bandleader Guy Lombardo's *Tempo VII*, an Allison-powered Les Staudacher creation, which was really on a roll that year. (Foster and crew chief Roy Duby had previously triumphed in the Copper Cup, the Silver Cup, the President's Cup and the International Cup.)

Tempo VII was a three-point prop-rider, a concept perfected in 1950 by the Ted Jones-designed *Slo-mo-shun IV*. The era of the fully submerged propeller now belonged to history. With only one fluke of the propeller in contact with the water at top speed, the boats rode much higher and were a whole lot faster. The semi-submerged propeller also accounted for the spectacular roostertail of spray that trailed behind the boat.

The Guy Lombardo team won all three heats of the 1955 Governor's Cup and simply outclassed second-place *Gale V*, co-driven by Lee Schoenith and Bill Cantrell.

Speeds were down at the 1956 Madison Regatta, but the reliability was extraordinary, with all five boats completing all three fifteen-mile heats. "Fearless Fred" Alter and the original *Miss U.S. I* placed second, first and first to claim the first of two Indiana Governor's Cup victories for owner George Simon of Detroit.

Bud Saile's twin-Allison-powered *Miss Wayne* took an overall second place and scored an unexpected victory in heat one by out-sprinting *Miss U.S. I* over the finish line by an incredible six feet. Third place in 1956 went to Doc Terry in Horace Dodge Jr.'s *Dora My Sweetie*, followed by Marv Henrich's *Wha Hoppen Too* (former *Gale II*) and Gordon Deneau's *What a Pickle* (former *Miss Cadillac*).

Record speeds and a record entry list highlighted the seventh annual running of the Indiana Governor's Cup in 1957. Jack Regas tore around the three-mile oval with Egar Kaiser's *Hawaii Kai III* at a 45-mile average of 106.061. The *Kai* was arguably the finest race boat of the 1950s and was the epitome of the all-conquering Ted Jones design.

Bob Schroeder was runner-up at the 1957 Madison Regatta with *Wildroot Charlie* (former *Gale IV*), while defending champion Fred Alter checked in third with a second-edition *Miss U.S. I*.

By far the most spectacular performance of the two-day event was achieved by Bill Muncey in the original *Miss Thriftway*. During heat 1-A on Saturday, September 28, the Willard Rhodes–owned entry turned an unprecedented 112.312 miles per hour, a world 15-mile competition mark that would stand for six years until 1963.

Following heat 2-A on Sunday, September 29, however, the newly crowned speed champion was a splintered wreck with its driver badly injured, following a 160-mile-an-hour disintegration at the start of lap two. It is speculated that a sponson, damaged the week before at a race in Washington, D.C., had not been adequately repaired. *Miss Wahoo* pilot Mira Slovak saw the accident, stopped his boat and went to the aid of the stricken Muncey.

Hydroplane Racing in Small-Town Indiana

The year 1957 was the first that the faster nationally ranked Seattle boats participated in the Madison Regatta. The *Kai*, the *Thriftway* and the *Wahoo* clearly represented the sport's upper echelon. Prior to 1957, no Unlimited hydroplane from west of the Mississippi River had ever competed at Madison.

The 1958 and 1959 Madison Regattas were lean years both in the number of participating boats and in the area of regatta finances. The amateur heyday was fast drawing to a close. The sponsoring organization would soon have to professionalize itself to survive.

When one less than the required minimum of four entries was received in 1958, industrialist Samuel F. DuPont came to the regatta's rescue with his new and unprepared *Nitrogen* from Wilmington, Delaware. With assistance from other boat crews, the DuPont craft not only started the race but finished with second-place points and scored a final heat victory with Bob Hayward at the wheel. Don Wilson and *Miss U.S. I* were the overall winners, followed by *Nitrogen*, Mira Slovak in *Miss Bardahl* and Bob Schroeder in *Wildroot Charlie*.

A quartet of challengers appeared for the 1959 Indiana Governor's Cup as well. The late, great Ron Musson, in his first season as an Unlimited hydroplane driver, won all three heats at an average speed of 102.939 aboard *Hawaii Kai III*, owned at this time by Joe Mascari of New York City. Musson is highly regarded as one of the top drivers of the piston era in Unlimited racing, although this would be his only victory at Madison. *Nitrogen* finished runner-up once again—this time with Norm Evans at the wheel—ahead of Bill Brow in *Miss Bardahl* and Bob Gilliam in *KOLroy*.

Helping out on the *Hawaii Kai III* crew at the 1959 Indiana Governor's Cup was Musson's good friend Graham Heath of Madison. Heath would later serve as crew chief of *Miss Madison* from 1961 to 1965 and of *My Gypsy* from 1966 to 1968.

THE SIXTIES

The Madison Regatta fell on hard times in the late 1950s. Due to a combination of circumstances, there almost was no race in 1960. Times were changing, and the regatta organization had to change with the times to survive.

The 1960s were a decade of change in Unlimited hydroplane racing. Cash prizes became mandatory. Boats with commercial names, rather than nicknames, became the rule rather than the exception.

Many Madisonians believed that the regatta was (in the words of past Regatta president Lyman Armstrong) "a dead duck."

About six weeks prior to the 1960 Indiana Governor's Cup, Phil Cole, Bob Snelling, Graham Taylor and other civic leaders formed the "Dead Duck Club." Almost overnight, the regatta had a new lease on life. The Dead Duck Club members regrouped, retrenched and secured a bank loan to put the organization back on a firm financial footing. Over twenty local civic groups and over 150 individual members all figured in the salvation of the Madison Regatta.

"A lot of old-timers went their separate ways in 1960," Cole admitted. "People like Birl Hill, who put a lot of himself into the regatta for many years, resisted the changes. I know that Birl was very bitter about what happened. But the restructuring was necessary for the regatta to survive."

And it did! The 1960 Indiana Governor's Cup race proved to be one of the more successful in regatta history. Bill Muncey and the third *Miss Thriftway* won it by a narrow margin over Bill Brow in *Miss Bardahl* and

Nitrogen Too.

Ron Musson in *Nitrogen Too*. From then on, the race would be run more as a business and less as a hobby.

Muncey became the first three-time consecutive winning driver of the Indiana Governor's Cup from 1960 to 1962 with *Miss Thriftway* (renamed *Miss Century 21* to publicize the 1962 Seattle World's Fair) during the same years that the famed Willard Rhodes craft won its trio of National Season Championships. So decisive was the Muncey-Rhodes domination that the persimmon-and-white U-60 entered nine heats at Madison, won eight of them and finished second once.

Ron Musson claimed the runner-up honors twice during the *Thriftway* era: in 1960 with *Nitrogen Too* and in 1962 with *Miss Bardahl*. These were both new boats in their first season of activity. Bill Cantrell took the second spot in 1961 with *Gale V* and was the only driver to ever defeat the victorious *Miss Century 21* in a heat of competition on the Ohio River.

The first—and to date the only—fatality in Madison Regatta history occurred in 1961. Hydroplane driver Jim Clark of Detroit was killed when he crashed Bob Ballinger's *Ballyhoo* in one of the heat races for the 266 Cubic Inch Class. A steering cable snapped on the fifteen-foot boat while speeding down the front straightaway at seventy-five miles per hour toward the first turn buoy. *Ballyhoo* rose up out of the water, came down hard, ripped off a sponson and flipped Clark into the river.

Not too long after the 1960 Madison Regatta, Phil Cole relocated to Washington, D.C., to join the staff of U.S. congressman Earl Wilson. Phil lived there for four years but remained a Madisonian at heart.

In those days, most of the active Unlimited hydroplanes headquartered in either Detroit or Seattle, with a few out of southern California. It was Cole's fondest wish that one of the so-called "Thunderboats" would someday call Madison, Indiana, home. He didn't have long to wait.

Cole was a good friend of Sam DuPont, who campaigned the *Nitrogen* and the *Nitrogen Too*. Madison had always been a favorite stop on the Unlimited tour for DuPont. When Sam retired from racing in the fall of 1960, Cole hinted that, by donating one of the boats to the City of Madison, he (DuPont) would qualify for a sizable tax deduction.

Phil's legendary powers of persuasion worked. In December 1960, the Ohio River town of thirteen thousand found itself to be the proud owner of a "Floating Chamber of Commerce." The former *Nitrogen*, an Allison-powered hydroplane built in 1957 by Les Staudacher, became the original *Miss Madison*.

Graham Heath was named crew chief for the 1961 season. When time permitted, Cole helped out as a member of the mechanical crew. Marion Cooper of Louisville was the driver. Other team members included Neal Cahall and Dick Cox, for whom Cooper had frequently driven in the 225 and 266 Inboard classes. Then there were Bob Humphrey, Ben Schnabel, Don Smith, Bob Neal and Don Tuite.

Nitrogen and Nitrogen Too.

The first race for the fledgling *Miss Madison* team was the 1961 Detroit Memorial Regatta, where they finished an overall fifth. Phil remembered how rough the racecourse was that day. "The holes in the Detroit River were so deep that, when a boat would fall into one of them, it would literally drop out of sight." Fortunately, Cooper had been racing on that river since the 1930s and was able to keep the *Miss M* together for all three heats. Later in the season, the team scored a hard-fought victory in the second-division Seattle Trophy Race at the Seafair World's Championship Regatta on Lake Washington.

The first *Miss Madison* made its initial appearance before the hometown crowd at the 1961 Madison Regatta. The former *Nitrogen* finished fourth in an eleven-boat field that first year and third in a ten-boat contingent in 1962. The team did a fine job making its presence felt in a sport dominated by millionaires.

The operating budget for the *Miss Madison* that year was minuscule. The volunteer crew had only one stock Allison engine, which had to last the entire season. The team couldn't afford any souvenir booster buttons, which the big-budget teams handed out in quantity. So the inimitable Cole had some *Miss Madison* decals printed up that read, "Stick on any *Miss Bardahl* button."

In 1963, Phil was instrumental in acquiring a second hull from his friend DuPont. Cole's original mission was to simply offer Sam $5,000 toward the purchase of some Allison engines. Lo and behold, Phil arrived back in Madison not only with the engines but also with the *Nitrogen Too* and the

Miss Madison (2).

entire DuPont equipment inventory—a package worth considerably more than the paltry $5,000 that changed hands. For the *Miss Madison* team, this was the deal of the century and one that served the city of Madison in good stead for many years to come.

The former *Nitrogen Too*, a 1959 Staudacher creation, made its first appearance in competition as the second *Miss Madison* at the 1963 Madison Regatta with George "Buddy" Byers as driver. This was the hull that went on to win the APBA Gold Cup on home waters in 1971 with Jim McCormick at the wheel.

Bill Brow emerged as Indiana Governor's Cup champion in 1963 with *Miss Exide*, owned by the Stoen brothers of Seattle. Brow had been toiling in the Unlimited ranks since 1958, but this was his first victory. *Miss Exide* was the former *Miss Wahoo*, which replaced an earlier *Miss Exide* that had disintegrated several weeks earlier at a race in Coeur d'Alene, Idaho, with Mira Slovak driving.

Bill Cantrell settled for another overall second-place with *Gale V* but established a Madison course record for the 45-mile distance on a 3-mile course with a reading of 106.867 miles per hour. *Miss Bardahl* ran third in 1963 with Don Wilson substituting for Ron Musson who had flipped the "Green Dragon" several days earlier during a practice run. Walt Kade finished fourth with *Blue Chip*, followed by Buddy Byers and the former *Nitrogen Too* in its first race as the second *Miss Madison*. (The original *Miss M* had struck floating debris and had been destroyed in a test run at the 1963 Gold Cup Regatta on the Detroit River with Morlan Visel as driver.)

Byers was one of the top 7-Litre Class drivers of his day. In 1960 at Madison, he and *Miss Desoto* had triumphed in the 7-Litre World Championship Race, sanctioned by the Union of International Motorboating (UIM) of Brussels, Belgium. Buddy went on to score the first major victory by the *Miss Madison* team in the Dixie Cup Regatta at Guntersville, Alabama, in 1965.

Bill Harrah of Reno, Nevada, became the second owner in four years to win three consecutive Indiana Governor's Cups. His *Tahoe Miss* proved to be the class of a thirteen-boat field in 1964, a fourteen-boat gathering in 1965 and a ten-boat contingent in 1966. Chuck Thompson claimed the first two victories, while his successor, Mira Slovak, tied down the third.

Runners-up to the casino-sponsored *Tahoe Miss* were Bill Cantrell once again with the new *Miss Smirnoff* in 1964, Ron Musson with *Miss Bardahl* in 1965, and Warner Gardner with *Miss Lapeer* in 1966.

Miss Madison finished third and sixth in 1964 and 1965 with Byers in the cockpit and took fourth during 1966 with rookie Jim McCormick at the wheel.

An accident involving "Wild Bill" Cantrell marred the 1965 Madison Regatta when *Miss Smirnoff* encountered the wake of an illegally moving

Miss Lapeer at the start of heat 2-A, after Cantrell had been victorious in Heat 1-A. Gardner and *Miss Lapeer* made a belated start from the pit area and left a sideways trough at right angles to the racecourse. *Miss Smirnoff* fell into that trough and pitched Bill out of the boat. Cantrell was badly hurt and spent many months in recovery. He returned to competition in 1966, but physically, he was never the same. Bill placed second in the 1966 Tri-Cities Atomic Cup at Kennewick, Washington, with the *Smirnoff* team but announced his retirement from driving in 1968. Inexplicably, no official action was ever taken against the errant Gardner.

Billy Schumacher made his first competitive appearance at the Madison Regatta in 1967 aboard the fifth *Miss Bardahl* with championship results—a feat that he duplicated the following year with the same boat. In both cases, "Billy the Schu" was the winner over thirteen other challengers on a racecourse shortened from three miles to two and a half miles in the interest of improving spectator vantage points.

Chuck Hickling took second place in 1967 with the former *Tahoe Miss*, renamed *Harrah's Club*, followed by Jim Ranger in *My Gypsy* and Jim McCormick in *Wayfarers Club Lady*. McCormick had arrived in town planning to drive Shirley Mendelson McDonald's *Notre Dame* but found himself replaced by Jack Regas. *Wayfarers Club Lady* owner Bob Fendler immediately "fired" himself as driver and installed McCormick in the *Wayfarers* cockpit. Fendler went on record with the media, blasting the *Notre Dame* organization for the insensitive manner in which McCormick was dismissed. (The *Notre Dame* people had come under similar fire when they replaced Bill Muncey with Rex Manchester at Madison in 1964.)

Warner Gardner and *Miss Eagle Electric* finished runner-up to *Miss Bardahl* in 1968. Bill Sterett Sr., in the new Ed Karelsen–designed *Miss Budweiser*—a virtual clone of the *Miss Bardahl*—took third place on points, followed by Jerry Schoenith in *Gale's Roostertail* and Jack Regas in *Notre Dame*.

The fastest heat of the day in 1968 was by Regas, who established a 15-mile Ohio River record for the smaller course at 104.026 that would stand for five years. During the final heat, Regas had *Notre Dame* in the lead for four laps and was two laps from victory when Schumacher and *Miss Bardahl* finally overtook them.

An added highlight of the 1968 Madison Regatta was the first of two contests for the Richard C. Heck Memorial Trophy, named after a recently deceased regatta past president. The one-heat race was for boats that did not qualify for the final heat of the Governor's Cup. Tommy "Tucker" Fults won the inaugural with *My Gypsy* and repeated in 1970 with *Pay 'n Pak's 'Lil Buzzard*.

The late 1960s were troubled times for Unlimited racing. A rash of fatalities shook the sport to its foundation. Three drivers (Ron Musson, Rex Manchester and Don Wilson) were lost in two separate accidents on the Potomac River at Washington, D.C., in 1966. Another (Chuck Thompson) was lost two weeks later at Detroit. Bill Brow was killed at Tampa, Florida, in 1967, followed by Warner Gardner at Detroit in 1968 and Tommy Fults at San Diego in 1970.

Madison, Indiana, was spared the specter of death when the Unlimiteds came to town to do competitive battle during those terrible years. This was before the introduction (in 1986) of the F-16 safety canopy, which is now mandatory on all of the big hydroplanes.

Dean Chenoweth, one of the most respected competitors in Unlimited history, followed Billy Schumacher's lead with a pair of back-to-back victories of his own at Madison in 1969 and 1970 at the controls of *Myr's Special* and *Miss Budweiser*.

Chenoweth had raced outboards at the Madison Regatta as early as 1952. Dean was a youthful spectator at Madison in 1954 when Bill Cantrell won the Indiana Governor's Cup with *Gale IV*. That particular race made a tremendous impression on Chenoweth: "It was like watching the World Series." Fifteen years later, Dean found himself as the Governor's Cup champion, astride a contemporary Gale Enterprises hull with none other than Cantrell as his team manager.

Bill Muncey was runner-up to Chenoweth at Madison in 1969 with *Miss U.S.* Muncey was at a "down" period in his life during the late 1960s. Since being fired off of *Notre Dame* in 1964, his career had not gone well. *Miss U.S.* was a problem boat with inadequate financing and had an alarming tendency to "fall on its nose" at high speeds. Bill's second-place finish at the 1969 regatta was one of his better performances.

Miss Madison placed third in the 1969 Indiana Governor's Cup with "Gentleman Jim" McCormick back in the cockpit, which had been occupied the two previous seasons by Ed O'Halloran. (*Miss M* had experienced considerable mechanical difficulty during 1967 and 1968. The team's best finish with O'Halloran driving was a second-place in the 1967 Tampa Suncoast Cup.)

The City of Madison had been in the Unlimited hydroplane racing business for twenty consecutive years. After starting out with a series of multi-class free-for-alls that didn't count for National High Points, the Madison Regatta was now a full-fledged Unlimited event. Only Detroit and Washington, D.C., which first appeared on the Unlimited calendar in 1946, had hosted more races than Madison.

THE SEVENTIES

B y the 1970s, the Unlimited hydroplanes were the showcase of the powerboat racing world and drew more spectators than any other category. The Unlimiteds had professionalized themselves into something more than just a rich man's hobby.

A landmark tax case in 1963, involving George Simon's *Miss U.S.* racing team, had far-reaching effects. The IRS had upheld Simon's contention that Unlimited racing was a legitimate business expense within specified guidelines and thereby tax deductible. This ruling opened the door to major corporate sponsorship of the Unlimiteds. One of the first companies to make a sizeable commitment to the sport on a national level was Anheuser-Busch, which introduced the first in a series of *Miss Budweiser* hydroplanes in 1964.

The Madison Regatta, after some anxious moments in the 1950s and 1960s, was solidly ensconced on the 1970s Unlimited tour and had its financial house in order. The first Indiana Governor's Cup of the new decade saw Dean Chenoweth repeat as champion with Bernie Little's *Miss Budweiser*. This was Little's first win at Madison. It would not be his last. Chenoweth had won the 1969 Governor's Cup with Joe Schoenith's *Myr's Special*.

Billy Sterett Jr. was the 1970 runner-up with *Miss Owensboro*, the former automotive-powered *Miss Chrysler Crew*, now empowered with an Allison engine borrowed from *My Gypsy*. Then came Leif Borgersen in *Notre Dame*, Bill Muncey in *Myr Sheet Metal* and Jim McCormick in *Miss Madison*. *Notre Dame* was an early leader in the 1970 Indiana Governor's Cup final heat until passed by Chenoweth on lap two. *Miss Madison* won preliminary heat

1-B but dropped from contention in the finale when it stalled, restarted and had to settle for fifth.

The following year would be a different story for the community-owned *Miss M.* Madison's sixtieth boat racing anniversary story in 1971 would amaze a fiction writer. That was when the community-owned *Miss Madison* won the race of races—the APBA Gold Cup—on the hometown racecourse before 110,000 partisan fans.

For the first time since 1951, the Indiana Governor's Cup took second billing to the Gold Cup, which had never in modern times been contested in so small a town. Due to a technicality and a misunderstanding, Madison's $30,000 bid for the race was the only one submitted to APBA headquarters in time.

For ten years, the volunteer *Miss M* crew had tried unsuccessfully to win the Madison race. Jim McCormick placed a crucial phone call to Reno, Nevada, and requested the assistance of two of the sport's finest Allison engine specialists: Harry Volpi and Everett Adams, who were former crew members of the now-inactive *Harrah's Club* team, for which McCormick had driven in 1968. Volpi and Adams worked alongside *Miss Madison* regulars Tony Steinhardt, Bob Humphrey, Dave Stewart, Keith Hand and Russ Willey at the 1971 Madison Regatta. Volpi and Adams helped to sort out the water-alcohol injection system, which resulted in some much-needed additional miles per hour for the *Miss Madison*.

The team faced an uphill fight in 1971. Their boat was eleven years old, and they were down to their last engine, after having blown the other during practice. Their one remaining power plant would have to carry the boat through all four fifteen-mile heats on that Fourth of July weekend.

McCormick and *Miss M* ran conservatively in their three preliminary heats and finished just high enough to qualify for the final moment of truth. Entering their last heat of the afternoon, McCormick and company had 1,000 points, based upon one first- and two second-place finishes. This compared to the 1,100-point total of Terry Sterett and *Atlas Van Liens II*, which had twice bested *Miss Madison* earlier in the day.

In order to win the Gold Cup, *Miss Madison* would have to win the final heat, with *Atlas Van Lines II* finishing second. That would put McCormick and Sterett in a point tie with 1,400 points apiece. According to Unlimited rules as they were written at the time, a tie in points would be broken by the order of finish in the final heat.

Miss Madison moved to the inside lane prior to the start. This forced the rest of the field to run a wider and longer track. *Atlas Van Lines II*, in lane two, crossed the starting line first and led around the first turn. *Miss Madison* took the lead on the first backstretch and streaked to victory with fast pursuit from *Atlas Van Lines II*, Dean Chenoweth in *Miss Budweiser*, Billy Schumacher in *Pride of Pay 'n Pak* and Fred Alter in *Towne Club*.

The hometown favorite received the checkered flag 16.3 seconds ahead of *Atlas Van Lines II*, adding a new chapter to American sports legend. In the words of radio announcer Jim Hendrick, "The town of Madison, Indiana, has gone absolutely wild!"

In truth, *Miss Madison* was not the thousand-to-one long shot of popular myth. Since late season 1970, *Miss M* had been a bona fide contender. But the timing of the victory on home waters—and in the most important race of the year—could not have been more perfect.

And to prove that the Gold Cup win was anything but a fluke, *Miss Madison* made it two in a row three weeks later when McCormick drove it to victory in the Tri-Cities Atomic Cup on the Columbia River at Kennewick, Washington.

Twenty-eight years later, *Madison*, a Hollywood motion picture, told the story of the 1971 Gold Cup with screen actor Jim Caviezel in the role of Jim McCormick.

Following 1971, the *Miss Madison* board of directors determined that the hull, which they had campaigned since 1963, was obsolete and needed to be retired. The boat had started in 162 heats and finished 150 of them.

Madison premiered in Madison, Indiana.

Two contemporary designs seemed to hold out considerable promise for the future in 1971. These were the *Atlas Van Lines*, co-designed by Bill Cantrell and Fred Dube of Gale Enterprises, and the *Pride of Pay 'n Pak*, designed by Ron Jones Sr. The *Atlas* had won at Washington, D.C., and Owensboro, Kentucky, in 1971. The *Pay 'n Pak*, on the other hand, had won the last three races of the 1971 season (at Seattle, Eugene and Dallas) and had raised the world lap speed record from 120 to 121 miles per hour on a 3-mile course (at Seattle). The *Miss Madison* team opted for an *Atlas Van Lines* hull and contracted with Gale Enterprises to build it for them.

Time would not vindicate the wisdom of the *Miss Madison* team's decision. The *Pride of Pay 'n Pak*—not the *Atlas Van Lines*—concept proved to be "the future of boat racing." The 1972 *Miss M* raced for six seasons and did not do badly but never won a race.

Madison Regatta, Inc., put in a bid to the APBA for the 1972 Gold Cup but lost out, this time to Detroit. Madison then applied for—and was granted—a sanction to host a World Championship Race for Unlimiteds, under the auspices of the Union of International Motorboating (UIM), in Brussels, Belgium.

The 1972 Madison Regatta, unfortunately and unlike 1971, proved to be a problem race. The flood-swelled and debris-filled Ohio River very nearly forced cancellation of the event, which was run on Independence Day instead of July 2 as originally planned. Qualifications had to be scrubbed, and Referee Ken Wright declared the race to be a contest after two sets of preliminary heats. No final heat was run. Joe Schoenith's *Atlas Van Lines* was declared the winner, based on decisive wins in heats 1-B and 2-B. This was the team's third Madison victory since 1954 and driver Bill Muncey's fourth since 1960.

Madison fans experienced disappointment in 1972 when the newly constructed third *Miss Madison* was unable to participate. Rookie driver Charlie Dunn had crashed the boat during a qualifying run at Detroit the week before, and it could not be repaired in time to compete at Madison.

Local fans did, however, have a chance to observe their boat in action during a postseason exhibition, which consisted of two three-boat heats, at Madison in October 1972. "Chargin' Charlie" Dunn wheeled the community-owned *Miss M* to second place behind Mickey Remund in *Lincoln Thrift's 7¼% Special* and ahead of Jim McCormick in *Miss Timex*.

After having been reduced to secondary status during 1971 and 1972, the Indiana Governor's Cup returned to the top of the shelf in 1973, where it would remain until the APBA Gold Cup returned to Madison in 1979 and 1980.

The 1973 race was a triumph for owner Dave Heerensperger and his new Ron Jones–designed *Pay 'n Pak*, nicknamed the "Winged Wonder," which utilized a unique horizontal stabilizer wing. This particular hull would become the fourth *Miss Madison* in 1978.

Pay 'n Pak driver Mickey Remund rewrote the record book at Madison in 1973 with new speed marks for lap, heat and race. He held off challenges from second-place Dean Chenoweth in *Miss Budweiser* and third-place Danny Walls in *Lincoln Thrift's 7¼ % Special*.

Heerensperger's team likewise won the 1974 and 1975 Indiana Governor's Cups with George Henley in the cockpit.

Chenoweth and *Miss Budweiser* again occupied the runner-up spot in 1974, while *Miss Madison* finished third with promising rookie driver Milner Irvin in the cockpit. Irvin would see intermittent duty with *Miss M* over the next decade. This was the year when the regatta had to be rescheduled from July to October, on account of tornado damage to many of the region's hotels and motels in April 1974.

One of the best all-around competitive boat races in Madison Regatta history occurred in 1975. Heerensperger's *Pay 'n Pak* team won their third consecutive Indiana Governor's Cup, but only after a titanic struggle with Billy Schumacher in Leslie Rosenberg's *Weisfield's* entry. Henley beat Schumacher over the finish line in heat 2-A at a record-breaking 115.148 miles per hour to 115.060 for the 12.5-mile distance.

The 1975 season in general can be summarized as the last hurrah—a glorious one—for the piston era in Unlimited racing. After thirty years of dependence on World War II fighter plane power sources, not enough good piston equipment remained to justify a class.

The Rolls-Royce Merlin was virtually extinct. The supply of Allisons was likewise dwindling. Automotive power had been tried but had—for the most part—proved wanting. For the next decade, it is difficult to point to a single season that matched the competitiveness of 1975. Not until the turbine revolution of the mid-1980s would the Unlimited Class of hydroplane have a new lease on life.

The 1976 Indiana Governor's Cup stands out as one of the more disappointing in the series. Only seven Unlimiteds attended on account of a particularly destructive race the week before in Detroit. Two prominent contenders, the *Miss Budweiser* and the *Olympia Beer*, had suffered major damage and weren't available to compete at Madison, although both teams were represented on the Ohio River by slower back-up hulls.

Atlas Van Lines and Bill Muncey simply outclassed second-place Tom D'Eath and *Miss U.S.* Muncey averaged 109.462 miles per hour in the final heat, compared to 105.783 for D'Eath. The year 1976 was the first in which the winner in all Unlimited races was determined not by total accumulated points but by the order of finish in the final heat.

The *Miss U.S.* racing team was accused of unsportsmanlike conduct at this race for refusing to run in preliminary heat 2-B, knowing that they already had enough points to qualify for the finale. With the non-participation of *Miss U.S.*, heat 2-B was reduced to a hopelessly one-sided exhibition, with *Atlas Van Lines* winning almost without opposition, thereby making a dull race even duller, much to the disappointment of the fans.

The most interesting heat of the day in 1976 was heat 2-A. *Miss Madison* driver Ron Snyder took first place after holding off a challenge from Tom Sheehy and the substitute *Miss Budweiser*.

The winning *Atlas Van Lines* was the phenomenal former *Pay 'n Pak* hull, which had emerged victorious at Madison in 1973, 1974 and 1975. This made the *Pak/Atlas* the most successful hydroplane in Madison Regatta history. No other boat before or since has ever won four Indiana Governor's Cups in a row.

A brand-new *Atlas Van Lines* appeared at Madison in 1977. This was the fabulously successful *Atlas Van Lines* "Blue Blaster," owned and driven by Muncey. Co-designed by Jim Lucero and Dixon Smith, the "Blue Blaster" became the first cabover (or forward-cockpit) hull to dominate in the Unlimited Class.

Atlas Van Lines won six out of nine races on the 1977 tour but had an off day at Madison. Muncey and *Atlas* had a fourth and a "Did Not Finish" in the preliminary action and didn't make the cut for the final heat of the Indiana Governor's Cup. The poor showing at Madison came back to haunt the "Blue Blaster" at season's end. The *Atlas* team fell 904 points short of the *Miss Budweiser* in National High Points.

The 1977 Governor's Cup victory went to the *Miss Bud* and driver Mickey Remund. *Budweiser* owner Bernie Little thus ended a seven-year dry spell at Madison. Second place went to Tom Sheehy in *Anheuser-Busch Natural Light*, also owned by Little. Then came third-place Ron Snyder in *Miss North Tool*.

Miss Madison took fourth at the 1977 Madison Regatta with rookie Jon Peddie in the cockpit. Peddie, a local body shop proprietor, is the only Madison resident to ever pilot a *Miss Madison* hydroplane in competition. (In 1999, driver Todd Yarling hailed from nearby Hanover, Indiana.) A veteran auto racer, Jon had never driven a hydroplane in his life when signed to pilot *Miss M.* Peddie readied himself for the assignment by test-driving Denny Jackson's *Ride-On*, a 280 Cubic Inch Class hydro. Jon went on to be honored as Unlimited Rookie of the Year in 1977.

The *Atlas Van Lines* team of owner/driver Muncey and crew chief Lucero rebounded from their lackluster 1977 Madison performance with a clear-cut victory in the 1978 Indiana Governor's Cup. They won hands-down; no one else was even close. This was in spite of losing the horizontal stabilizer in heat 1 and suffering hull damage to the port side in a subsequent heat.

Second place at the 1978 Madison Regatta went to the *Squire Shop*, owned by Seattleite Bob Steil and driven by twenty-four-year-old Lee "Chip" Hanauer. This was Chip's first appearance at Madison. In 1982, Hanauer would replace Muncey as *Atlas Van Lines* driver after Bill was fatally injured in the last race of the 1981 season with the "Blue Blaster" at Acapulco, Mexico.

The seventh and final victory by Bill Muncey at Madison occurred in 1979, which was a Gold Cup year. Ten teams gathered to do competitive battle for powerboat racing's crown jewel. These included a promising trio of new hulls: the Rolls-Royce Griffon-powered *Miss Budweiser*, designed by Ron Jones Sr., and a couple of Rolls-Royce Merlin boats from the drawing board of Dave Knowlen. These were the *Squire Shop* and *Miss Circus Circus*. The new boats were expected to provide meaningful competition for the all-conquering *Atlas Van Lines*. And they did. But the "Blue Blaster" still prevailed at Madison.

The Ohio River was extremely rough on race day in 1979. Going into the first turn of the final heat, *Miss Circus Circus* landed in a deep "hole." Driver Steve Reynolds was almost flipped out of the boat, and his foot came off the throttle. The boat stalled, but Reynolds managed to restart the engine and took off after the front-running *Atlas*. But by then, Muncey's lead was insurmountable. *Atlas Van Lines* took the checkered flag a full mile ahead of *Miss Circus Circus*, followed by Chip Hanauer in the *Squire Shop*.

Bill Muncey was to boat racing what Babe Ruth was to baseball—the sport's most celebrated participant. Muncey was fifty years old at the 1979 Madison Regatta and had twenty-seven months to live.

The current series of Madison races had come a long way since its humble 1949 origin. The regatta—and its all-volunteer committee—had elevated the tiny municipality to the national sports arena.

THE EIGHTIES

The 1980s was a decade of change for Unlimited hydroplane racing. The most significant changes were in the areas of power sources and safety equipment.

Since the end of World War II, the APBA Unlimited Class had depended largely upon government surplus fighter aircraft engines—most notably the G.M. Allison and the Packard Rolls-Royce Merlin. But by the late 1970s, these were in short supply.

Seven Unlimited drivers lost their lives in the 1960s, followed by three more in the 1970s. And in the 1980s, Bill Muncey of *Atlas Van Lines* fame was fatally injured in a race at Acapulco, Mexico, in October 1981. Dean Chenoweth of *Miss Budweiser* perished nine months later on the Columbia River in the Tri-Cities, Washington.

In the words of one critic, "The sport must be made safer and safer, not just faster and faster." It would take a few years for these concerns to be worked out. In the meantime, the racers proceeded with business as usual and put on some pretty impressive shows for the spectators.

The 1980 Madison Regatta, which featured the APBA Gold Cup, was especially memorable. Four of the five entrants (all except for *Miss Budweiser*) jumped the gun in the final heat, and *Budweiser*'s Chenoweth believed that he had done likewise. (This was in the days before drivers had radio communication with their crews.)

Muncey in *Atlas Van Lines* and Steve Reynolds in *Miss Circus Circus* led down the first back straightaway along the Kentucky shore with the "Beer

Wagon" in hot pursuit. *Budweiser* passed *Circus* after three-quarters of a lap and then took off after *Atlas*. *Miss Budweiser* caught up with *Atlas Van Lines* on the third of five laps and passed Muncey on the outside. Chenoweth and the Rolls-Royce Griffon-powered *Bud* went on to claim the checkered flag and the Gold Cup in championship fashion. The spectator throng was on its feet and roared its approval. It was the kind of race that brings crowds back.

"Dapper Dean" made it two in a row in 1981 with the Griffon *Miss Budweiser*. The Indiana Governor's Cup was one of six race victories claimed by the *Bud* camp that year. Chenoweth also turned the first-ever lap at over 130 miles per hour in Madison Regatta history with a clocking of 130.058 during qualification around the narrow 2.5-mile oval course.

Miss Budweiser ran away from the field in the winner-take-all final heat. *Miss Madison* took second place, with Milner Irvin at the wheel.

Bill Muncey, the winningest Unlimited driver of them all, in his final Madison appearance, concluded the day at the end of a towrope when his *Atlas Van Lines* "Blue Blaster" failed to finish due to mechanical difficulties.

For ten years, between 1972 and 1981, all of the Governor's Cup winners coincidentally emerged as the National High Point Champions for the years in question. That tradition did not hold true in 1982. The *Squire Shop*, which went on to finish third in National Points, would not be denied on race day at Madison. Although somewhat down on power, *Squire Shop* pilot Tom D'Eath made a picture-perfect start in the final heat and led from wire to wire. *Miss Madison*, driven this year by Ron Snyder, took second place for the second year in a row. Another local favorite, *Miss Kentuckiana Paving*, driven by Madisonian Jon Peddie and co-owned by Bill Cantrell and Graham Heath, overtook an ailing *Miss Budweiser* on the final lap of the race and finished third.

The new *Atlas Van Lines*, owned by Fran Muncey (Bill's widow) and driven by Chip Hanauer, went on to be National Champion in 1982 but failed to finish at Madison.

The 1983 Indiana Governor's Cup was officially designated as the "Dean Chenoweth Memorial Race" by Madison Regatta, Inc., in honor of the late champion who had won the Madison race four times between 1969 and 1981. Fittingly enough, the Governor's Cup winner in 1983 was none other than Chenoweth's handpicked successor, Jim Kropfeld, who guided the *Miss Budweiser* to victory in all three heats. Kropfeld defeated second-place Hanauer and *Atlas Van Lines* in the final heat. *Miss Bud* also broke a course record that had been established by Chenoweth with a competition lap of 128.202 in the final heat.

Although no one could have known it at the time, 1983 was the last year that the Madison race would be attended by an all-piston fleet. The Griffon *Miss Budweiser* was the last Governor's Cup winner to use an internal combustion engine. The turbine revolution, which had been predicted for decades, finally happened in 1984. In most instances, this took the form of a Lycoming T-55 L-7 power plant, originally intended for use in the Vietnam-era Chinook helicopter.

Three teams—Fran Muncey's *Atlas Van Lines*, Steve Woomer's *Miss Tosti Asti* and Bob Taylor's *Lite All-Star*—all climbed on the turbine bandwagon in 1984. And Unlimited racing hasn't been the same since.

After forty years of domination, the time-honored Allison and Rolls-Royce Merlin would soon go the way of the biplane and the Model T Ford. For the sport to survive, the "thunder" had to go out of the Thunderboats.

The first turbine winner of the Indiana Governor's Cup was *Atlas Van Lines*, piloted by Chip Hanauer, in 1984. The "Awesome *Atlas*" simply annihilated the opposition. *Miss Budweiser*, the 1983 champion, was a distant runner-up.

Turbine-powered boats had tried their luck in the Unlimited Class before. These included most prominently Jim Clapp's *U-95* in 1973–74 and Dave Heerensperger's *Pay 'n Pak* in 1980–82. But *Atlas Van Lines* was the first truly competitive turbine craft that could hold its own against any piston boat in the world.

There could be no doubt about it. The turbine era had most assuredly begun.

The second turbine winner of the Madison race was *Miss 7-Eleven* (formerly *Miss Tosti Asti*) in 1985. Driver Steve Reynolds finished first, second and first to score the victory over second-place Scott Pierce in *Executone* and third-place Jerry Hopp in *Oh Boy! Oberto*.

The former *Atlas Van Lines* (renamed *Miller American*) had been favored to repeat as Indiana Governor's Cup champion, after having qualified at a record-breaking 140.100 miles per hour. Mechanical gremlins, however, plagued pilot Hanauer on race day and prevented him from participating in the final heat.

But there would be no stopping "Champion Chip" in 1986. *Miller American* won all four Governor's Cup heats to dominate the racing action. Jim Kropfeld and the *Miss Budweiser*/Turbine-1 gave Hanauer a good battle in heat 3-B and the final heat. But there could be no denying that this was "Chip Hanauer Day" on the Ohio River. This was in spite of the unexplained departure of *Miller American* crew chief Jim Lucero a few weeks prior to the start of the 1986 season. The *Miller* team had performed badly at the season-opener in Miami, but they clearly had their act together at Madison.

Spectators at the 1986 Madison race caught their first glimpse of a new technical innovation that would revolutionize the Unlimited Class. Both the *Miss Budweiser*/Turbine-1 and the *Miss 7-Eleven* were safety-equipped with an F-16 jet fighter plane canopy. The egg-shaped canopies had been installed by famed designer Ron Jones Sr. Beginning in 1987, all new Unlimited hydroplanes were required to use the F-16 canopy; the older boats were given until 1989 to make the change-over.

Since the introduction of the safety canopy, only one fatality has occurred in Unlimited racing (George Stratton at San Diego in 2000). Over the past quarter-century, drivers have literally walked away from accidents that most certainly would have been fatal in earlier times.

The 1987 Madison Regatta is one that most people would rather forget. The Governor's Cup was won by Jim Kropfeld and the new super-fast *Miss Budweiser*/Turbine-2. But what everyone remembers is the tragic accident that involved popular Steve Reynolds, the 1985 Madison winner.

Reynolds and *Cellular One* were leading Kropfeld and *Miss Budweiser* on lap one of heat 3-A when disaster struck. *Cellular One* (formerly *Miss 7-Eleven*) became airborne, blew over backward and crashed violently near the Kentucky shore. Kropfeld just narrowly avoided a collision. Rescue crews found Steve unconscious in the cockpit. He was airlifted to Indianapolis Methodist Hospital with head trauma and other injuries.

The *Cellular One* crew had rebuilt the boat during the off-season, but they had not tested it. At the race in Evansville, Indiana, the week prior to Madison, the boat demonstrated an alarming tendency to become airborne at high speeds. This problem was not corrected in time for the Madison race.

Reynolds spent the next few years in recovery. The F-16 safety canopy, installed the year before, was credited with saving Steve's life.

If 1987 was a "downer," the 1988 Madison race was definitely an "upper" with lots of competitive action for the fans. Driver Scott Pierce and owner Bill Wurster took the top prize with *Mr. Pringle's*. Wurster had been bringing boats to Madison since 1978 without success.

The best duel of the day occurred in heat 1-A. Larry Lauterbach and *Competition Specialties* battled head to head with Pierce and *Mr. Pringle's* for three dynamic laps. Lauterbach posted the fastest heat speed of the day with a clocking of 129.752 to Pierce's 129.369.

The 1989 Indiana Governor's Cup almost didn't happen on account of flood conditions. Fortunately, the Ohio River cooperated and the race was run as scheduled.

Jim Kropfeld, after having missed much of the 1988 season because of a fractured vertebra at Miami, was his old victorious self at Madison in 1989. "King Kropfeld" captured his third Governor's Cup since 1983 with a four-heat grand slam in the new *Miss Budweiser*/Turbine-3.

The final heat was a thriller with the field closely bunched at the start. *Miss Bud* stayed close to the buoy line, took the lead coming out of the first turn and proceeded on to victory with fast pursuit from George Woods in *Oh Boy! Oberto*, Pierce in *Mr. Pringle's*, Hanauer in *Miss Circus Circus* and Lauterbach in *Winston Eagle*.

The best driver news of the 1989 Madison Regatta was the encouraging progress of Steve Reynolds. Steve returned to Madison for the first time since his near-fatal 1987 crash. He appeared in good spirits and had clearly come a long way on the road to recovery.

THE NINETIES

By the 1990s, the APBA Unlimited Class was predominantly a turbine class. All ten of the Indiana Governor's Cup winners at the Madison Regatta used Lycoming turbine power. The most victorious team at Madison during the decade of the nineties was Bernie Little's *Miss Budweiser*, which won five times with drivers Chip Hanauer and Dave Villwock. Hanauer emerged as the winningest driver at Madison during the nineties. He achieved five victories with *Miss Circus Circus*, *Miss Budweiser* and *Miss Pico*.

The 1990 season featured a titanic struggle for National Championship honors between two top teams—*Miss Circus Circus* with Hanauer and *Miss Budweiser* with Tom D'Eath. *Circus Circus* won six races that year and *Budweiser* won five. Hanauer's team finally clinched the title on the last day of the season (at Las Vegas).

Miss Circus Circus scored a come-from-behind victory at the 1990 Madison Regatta. *Miss Budweiser* led out of the first turn in the winner-take-all final heat with *Miss Circus Circus* close behind. The *Budweiser* then struck a roller, became airborne and almost capsized. The *Budweiser* came back down and continued on in a distant second place, despite serious damage to the right sponson. *Circus Circus* had a decisive lead at the end of lap one and was never headed.

The 1990 season featured a lot of action for the fans. At long last, here was someone who could provide meaningful competition for the long-dominant *Miss Budweiser*. But no sooner had the season concluded when *Miss Circus Circus* owner Bill Bennett stunned the racing world by announcing his retirement from competition. For the second time, since first entering the sport in 1978, Bennett had put together a winning combination with some truly top-flight personnel and then thrown it all away. No believable explanation was ever put forth for this bizarre turn of events, but there could be no doubt as to the outcome. The sport had lost one of its major players.

Within a matter of days, *Winston Eagle* owner Steve Woomer stepped forward and purchased the entire *Miss Circus Circus* inventory of hulls and equipment. The hull that had won the 1990 Indiana Governor's Cup became the "new" *Winston Eagle*.

A brand-new Unlimited hydroplane team in only its third race appearance took first place at the 1991 Madison Regatta. Joining the ranks of Unlimited owners in 1991 was Ron Jones Jr., a third-generation boat racer from Seattle. Using a seven-year-old hull borrowed from Steve Woomer (the former 1984 Atlas *Van Lines*), the young Jones and his *American Spirit* team raised many eyebrows by qualifying for five final heats in a row in 1991 with Mark Evans driving.

In the final heat at Madison, Evans and *American Spirit* were physically second after Mark Tate and the front-running *Winston Eagle* were penalized for "chopping" Scott Pierce and *Miss Budweiser* in the first turn.

Miss Madison, sponsored by Valvoline and driven by Mike Hanson, finished runner-up in the 1991 Indiana Governor's Cup. This was the *Miss M*'s first hometown appearance with Lycoming turbine power, after having used Allison reciprocal engines exclusively since 1961.

The next three Madison Regattas in a row all belonged to *Miss Budweiser* and new driver Chip Hanauer. Chip had sat out the 1991 season, following the retirement of the *Miss Circus Circus* team, but signed with Bernie Little's *Miss Budweiser* in 1992. This came as a surprise to many fans. "It's true that Bernie and I have been intense rivals in the past," Hanauer acknowledged. "But as much as I tried to surpass Bernie, I'll be working just as hard for him—as the driver of the *Miss Budweiser*."

Finishing second to Chip at each of the 1992–94 Governor's Cup races was the former *Miss Circus Circus* that Hanauer had driven for Bill Bennett. Renamed *Winston Eagle* in 1992 and 1993 *and Smokin' Joe's* in 1994, Chip's former mount—now driven by Mark Tate—was always in the hunt.

The community-owned *Miss Madison*, sponsored by Kellogg's Frosted Flakes, placed fourth at the Madison Regatta in both 1992 and 1993 but was without a sponsor the following year. Not wishing to see the demise of a thirty-three-year tradition, Powerball Lottery contributed some sponsorship dollars. In the team's only 1994 race appearance, Mike Hanson steered the *Miss M* to fifth place in the Indiana Governor's Cup.

After three consecutive second-place finishes at the Madison Regatta in previous years, Mark Tate finally achieved the top of the podium in both 1995 and 1996 with *Smokin' Joe's*. Tate's major competition during those years was *Miss Budweiser* pilot Mark Evans.

In 1995, Tate and *Smokin' Joe's* led from the first turn onward in the final heat. Evans and *Miss Budweiser* spun out in the first turn. Mike Hanson and *Miss Madison* (alias *Miss Jasper Engines & Transmissions*) chased *Smokin' Joe's* for a couple of laps and was one roostertail length behind *Smokin' Joe's* when the restarting *Miss Budweiser* pulled directly in front of *Miss Madison* and caused *Miss M* to spin out and go dead in the water. *Miss Budweiser* was disqualified for this action. *Miss Madison* restarted and managed to finish fifth, despite extensive damage to its right rear.

Future *Miss Madison* pilot Steve David was involved in a frightening mishap during heat 1-B of the 1995 Madison Regatta. While driving Jim Harvey's *T-Plus Engine Treatment*, David crossed the starting line first and was leading by a boat length at the entrance to the first turn when the boat became airborne and blew over, landing upside down. Fortunately, the *T-Plus* was not seriously damaged and Steve suffered only bruises.

Steven David.

T-Plus Engine Treatment.

In 1996, Tate and *Smokin' Joe's* defended their Indiana Governor's Cup title in championship fashion with victories in all four heats. The final heat was a classic. At the end of lap one, *Smokin' Joe's*, *Miss Budweiser* and *Pico American Dream* with Dave Villwock were virtually dead even, with *Smokin' Joe's* slightly ahead. *Miss Budweiser* fell slightly off the pace on lap two while *Smokin' Joe's* and *Pico* continued to fight it out for the lead. Tate led Villwock by one and a half roostertails after lap three. Villwock then lost power in the first turn of lap four. Evans caught up with Villwock and took over second place. Villwock restarted and went on to take third.

Miss Budweiser returned to the Madison Regatta winner's circle in 1997—this time with Villwock in the cockpit. (Dave had been hired as driver and team manager of the Bernie Little team, while Mark Evans took over Villwock's previous assignment with *Pico American Dream*.) In the final heat of the 1997 Governor's Cup, *Pico* and *Budweiser* exited the first turn together and charged head to head down the backstretch. In the second turn of lap one, *Pico* appeared not to hold its lane and slid into *Budweiser's* roostertail. *Pico* then went dead in the water. Nate Brown quickly moved into second place with *Miss Truckgear* but was unable to overtake the front-running *Miss Budweiser*.

The Madison Regatta was one of four consecutive race victories by Villwock and *Miss Bud* during the first half of the 1997 season. That string came to an abrupt end at the Tri-Cities (Washington) Columbia Cup when

"Super Dave" had a very serious injury accident that almost ended his racing career. The boat blew over in the first turn of the final heat, and Villwock suffered the loss of two fingers on his right hand.

At the outset of 1998, the burning question was whether Dave Villwock still had what it took to drive an Unlimited hydroplane safely and competitively. During the 1997–98 off-seasons, Dave underwent physical therapy and no fewer than sixteen surgeries on his right hand. Fortunately, Dave is left-handed.

When the checkered flag dropped at the first race of 1998 in Evansville, Indiana, Villwock was the winner. It was as if he had never been away. The *Miss Budweiser* team won not only the Evansville race but eight out of ten races on the 1998 Unlimited tour as well, including the Governor's Cup at Madison.

In the final heat of the 1998 Madison Regatta, Mark Evans and *Pico American Dream* led *Miss Budweiser* into the first turn. On the second turn of lap one, *Pico* pushed *Budweiser* into an outer course marker, which resulted in a one-lap penalty for *Pico American Dream*. Evans physically stayed ahead of Villwock for two and a half laps but was passed by Villwock on lap three. *Miss Budweiser* then pulled away to a decisive lead. Ken Muscatel and *Miss Northwest Unlimited* was physically third—but officially second—in the corrected order of finish.

Mike Hanson, in his final appearance as *Miss Madison* driver, steered the community-owned craft to an overall third place in the 1998 Indiana Governor's Cup. In later years, Mike would return to *Miss Madison* as the team's crew chief.

The 1999 Indiana Governor's Cup almost didn't happen. Madison Regatta, Inc., the sponsoring organization, was in serious financial trouble. Flooding of the Ohio River had forced a last-minute postponement of the 1998 race from the traditional Fourth of July date to Labor Day weekend. The expected large crowd did not materialize.

Incoming Madison Regatta president Denny Jackson inherited an almost untenable situation. Corporate sponsorship was needed—and in a hurry— to save the event. Jackson managed to negotiate a deal with Jasper Engines & Transmissions of Jasper, Indiana, which allowed the tradition of Unlimited hydroplane racing in Madison to continue.

The 1999 Madison Regatta, with its new financial lease on life, proved popular with the fans. Chip Hanauer ended a three-year retirement from competition as driver for Fred Leland's *Miss Pico* team. And he won the race! In so doing, Hanauer came back to haunt his former *Miss Budweiser* teammates by claiming his seventh Governor's Cup title since 1982 and his fifth in the decade of the 1990s.

Heading into the first turn of the final heat, *Miss Pico* had the lead. The heat was stopped moments later when Dave Villwock and *Miss Budweiser* became airborne and flipped. Villwock was uninjured but, having caused the stoppage, was ineligible for the restart, which was won by Hanauer at 133.351 miles per hour, compared to 132.297 for second-place Mitch Evans and *Appian Jeronimo*.

The 1999 Indiana Governor's Cup would prove to be "Champion Chip's" final appearance on the Madison racecourse. At season's end, Hanauer announced his retirement—this time for good. Chip had first appeared at the Madison Regatta in 1978 as pilot for the *Squire Shop* when he was twenty-four years old. At age forty-five, Hanauer had sixty-one victories in the Unlimited Class and decided to call it a career.

THE TWENTY-FIRST CENTURY

As the twenty-first century dawned, Bernie Little's *Miss Budweiser* would not be denied. Owner Little, driver/team manager Dave Villwock and crew chief Mark Smith claimed a twentieth National High Point Championship for sponsor Anheuser-Busch in 2000. This was on the strength of six victories in seven races, including the Indiana Governor's Cup at Madison, on the Unlimited Hydroplane Series tour. *Miss Budweiser*'s only defeat occurred at the Tri-Cities, Washington, Columbia Cup. That was when damage suffered during a collision with another boat in a preliminary heat forced the *Bud* to withdraw.

At Detroit in 2000, the *Miss Budweiser* team set an Unlimited Class record for consecutive race wins with ten in a row—the last six of 1999 and the first four of 2000. That broke Bill Muncey's long-standing mark of nine victories with *the Atlas Van Lines* "Blue Blaster" during 1978 and 1979.

In the final heat of the 2000 Madison Regatta, Villwock and *Miss Budweiser* led out of the first turn and immediately pulled away to a commanding lead. Mark Weber settled into a steady but distant second place with *York Heating and Air Conditioning*, followed by Mike Hanson in *Jones Racing*, George Stratton in *Appian Jeronimo* and Jimmy King in *Llumar Window Film*.

Fourth-place finisher Stratton appeared to be on the threshold of a long and successful career in the Unlimited ranks. He had already clinched the Rookie of the Year title for 2000 when he was tragically lost in a "blow-over" accident at San Diego during a test run on the last day of the season. A gust of wind caused the *Appian*'s bow to pitch skyward. The boat landed upside-down. Stratton is believed to have died instantly. This was the first loss of life in the Unlimited Class since Dean Chenoweth's fatality in 1982 at the Tri-Cities with *Miss Budweiser*. This was also the first death to occur since the introduction in 1986 of the F-16 safety canopy, which has been credited with saving numerous lives in Unlimited racing.

The community-owned *Miss Madison* used three drivers during 2000. Charley Wiggins, a promising rookie, newly recruited from the Unlimited Light Class, suffered injuries at Evansville and Detroit and resigned from the team. Jerry Hopp replaced Wiggins (with fifteen minutes notice!) at Detroit and guided *Miss M* to fifth place in the Gold Cup. Nate Brown was hired for the West Coast races, where he finished third at the Tri-Cities and San Diego and fourth at Seattle under the sponsorship of *Oh Boy! Oberto*. The Seattle-based Oberto Meat Products firm would remain as the primary *Miss Madison* racing team sponsor for the next decade.

Steve David.

Oh Boy! Oberto/Miss Madison.

Heading into 2001, Miss Madison, Inc., president Bob Hughes announced the hiring of Steve David as the nineteenth driver for the team since 1961. One of the sport's most respected competitors, David would go on to be the winningest driver in *Miss Madison* team history, with nine race victories between 2001 and 2010, three National High Point Team Championships and five National High Point Driver Championships.

Unlimited hydroplane fans had caught their first glimpse of Steve when he was 1988 Rookie of the Year with Jim McCormick's *Pocket Savers Plus*. David had a successful career with the Jim Harvey Motorsports team throughout the 1990s but had been inactive in the Unlimited Class since 1999. It didn't take Steve long to regain his winning ways.

At the second race of the 2001 Unlimited season, Steve David and *Oh Boy! Oberto/Miss Madison* took first place in the Indiana Governor's Cup before the hometown crowd. This hadn't happened in thirty years. Steve made a perfect on-the-nose start in the winner-take-all final heat, while three other boats "jumped the gun" and incurred a one-lap penalty. For five heart-pounding laps, *Oh Boy! Oberto* held off a dynamic challenge from second-place *Zenetix* and Greg Hopp, who forced David to work for it every inch of the way to the checkered flag and victory. The front-page headline of the *Madison Courier* the following day summed it all up in just two words: "Oh Boy!"

Nate Brown ruled the roost at the 2002 Madison Regatta as driver of *Miss E-Lam Plus*, owned by the Ellstrom family of Seattle. Brown rebounded from having to run a penalty lap in heat 1-A for jumping the gun and went on to win his next three heats in fine fashion. Nate trailed Terry Troxell and *Miss Troxzilla* for two and three-quarter laps in the final heat before overtaking Troxell and pulling to a commanding lead on lap four.

Brown was really on a roll in 2002. This was his third victory in four consecutive races on the Unlimited tour. Nate had won the final two races of the 2001 season at Seattle and San Diego with the Ellstrom team.

Miss Budweiser and driver Dave Villwock once again achieved the top of the podium at the 2003 Madison Regatta. Not even the death of *Miss Budweiser* team founder Bernie Little on April 25, 2003, could derail the "Beer Wagon's" competitive momentum. Joe Little picked up where his late father had left off and guided *Miss Budweiser* to its twenty-third National High Point Championship since 1969.

Villwock piloted *Miss Budweiser* to first place in all four heats of the 2003 Indiana Governor's Cup. The final heat had to be restarted following an accident involving *Miss Emcor* and driver Mike Weber. In the rerun, Villwock led Mark Evans and *Llumar Window Film* by one and a half roostertails after lap one and then pulled away to a decisive lead.

The 2004 Unlimited hydroplane season shaped up as a farewell tour for the legendary *Miss Budweiser*, which ended its involvement with the Unlimiteds after forty-two years of participation. At season's end, the Anheuser-Busch-sponsored team had five victories in seven races and notched one final Madison Regatta win, which carried with it the World Championship label, sanctioned by the Union of International Motorboating (UIM).

Dave Villwock and *Miss Budweiser* once again dominated the racing action by winning all four Governor's Cup heats. Greg Hopp and *Marian Travel Inn* were a distant second in the final heat, with Terry Troxell taking third with *Miss E-Lam Plus*.

The retirement of Anheuser-Busch signified not only the loss of *Miss Budweiser* from the starting lineup in 2005 but also the loss of Budweiser beer as title sponsor for the Madison Regatta. But that didn't deter the local committee, which put on another top-notch Indiana Governor's Cup event and turned a profit in so doing.

The final heat of the 2005 Governor's Cup saw Jimmy King and the Allison-powered *Master Tire* lead out of the first turn, followed closely by J.W. Myers and *Miss E-Lam Plus*. Myers passed King at the end of lap one and pulled away on lap two. King ran one to two roostertails behind Myers the rest of the way. Jean Theoret and *Llumar Window Film* battled with Steve David and *Oh Boy! Oberto/Miss Madison* for third place for four laps with *Llumar* maintaining a slight edge over *Oberto* when *Llumar* conked out at the start of lap five.

Long touted as one of Unlimited racing's most talented prospects, J.W. Myers made a strong impression at Madison, winning all four of his heats and propelling *Miss E-Lam Plus* into the National High Point lead.

The Madison Regatta committee members did themselves proud in 2005, despite the lack of a title sponsor. They were honored at season's end as "Race Site of the Year" by the sanctioning American Boat Racing Association (ABRA).

Following the success of the 2005 Regatta, everyone expected the upward favorable trend to continue into 2006. Unfortunately, that proved not to be the case, for well-known tragic reasons.

In the long history of Unlimited hydroplane racing, few races have proved more catastrophic than the fifty-sixth running of the Indiana Governor's Cup. For openers, the Ohio River would not cooperate in 2006. Flood conditions forced cancellation of testing and qualifying on the Saturday of Madison Regatta race week. The boats finally took to the water on Sunday morning. One craft after another was forced to withdraw on account of damage caused mostly by floating debris. *Oh Boy! Oberto/Miss Madison* lost a rudder and spun violently into the infield at the start of heat 2-B, narrowly missing the flag boat anchored inside the racecourse. Driver Steve David, fortunately, escaped injury.

Then, with the clock counting down to the scheduled start of the final heat, the unthinkable occurred. An errant automobile, driven by an intoxicated eighteen-year-old male, crashed through the security gates, plowed through the spectator throng and came to a stop in the Ohio River. A total of fourteen serious injuries sent the rescue crews, normally used for the Regatta, into lifesaving action. Two of the victims were injured critically.

Madison mayor Al Huntington announced cancellation of the final heat. *Miss E-Lam Plus* and driver Dave Villwock were declared the Governor's

Oh Boy! Oberto/Miss Madison.

Cup winners on the basis of points earned in the preliminary heats. But no one felt like celebrating. And the 2006 Madison Regatta went down as one of the most frustrating and saddest in racing history.

After the heartbreak of 2006, the 2007 Madison Regatta was a much-needed pick-me-up. The first new *Miss Madison* since 1988 made its debut in 2007. The new *Miss M*, sponsored by Oh Boy! Oberto, was an instant contender, co-designed by Dale VanWieringen, Ron Jones Jr. and crew chief Mike Hanson.

Miss E-Lam Plus made it three Indiana Governor's Cup victories in a row in 2007, but it wasn't a clean sweep for the Ellstrom team. The new *Oh Boy! Oberto/Miss Madison* defeated *Miss E-Lam Plus* in preliminary heat 1-A. "He [Steve David] beat me fair and square in Heat 1-A," admitted *E-Lam* driver Villwock. "That's racing. In the end, I was able to beat him. But what he did today was amazing. This was a great race."

David and *Oh Boy! Oberto* won all three of their elimination heats to garner a spot on the front row for the final heat at Madison. But it was defending champion Villwock who was able to pull away from David on lap two of the five-lap race. Villwock averaged 139.641 miles per hour to David's 137.684, followed by J. Michael Kelly and *Spirit of Detroit* at 132.634.

By season's end, *Oh Boy! Oberto* was second to *Miss E-Lam Plus* in 2007 National High Points. Driver Steve David scored back-to-back victories in the Chevrolet Cup at Seattle and the Bill Muncey Cup at San Diego.

Competition was the key word to describe Unlimited hydroplane action in 2008. There was plenty of it, and no one team won a majority of races.

Ellstrom's *Miss E-Lam Plus* and *Oh Boy! Oberto* in the 2007 Madison race.

When the roostertails subsided after the last race of the season on San Diego's Mission Bay, *Oh Boy! Oberto/Miss Madison* (U-6) had first place in National High Points for the first time in its forty-eight-year history. This entitled the U-6 to carry the coveted U-1 designation in 2009.

The community-owned craft from southern Indiana and driver Steve David had 4,764 accumulated points, compared to 4,146 for *Formulaboats. com* (U-5) and Jeff Bernard and 3,934 for *Miss Beacon Plumbing* (U-37) and Jean Theoret.

Oh Boy! OBerto achieved 100 percent reliability in 2008 and finished every heat entered. The U-6 qualified fastest at four of the six events and won the Tri-Cities Columbia Cup. It finished second in its hometown Indiana Governor's Cup at Madison.

The defending National High Point Championship team of *Miss E-Lam Plus* and driver Dave Villwock followed a reduced schedule in 2008 and appeared at only the two Washington state races but did manage a victory in the Chevrolet Cup at Seattle.

Victory at the 2008 Madison Regatta went to *Formulaboats.com* (U-5). The *Formula* team—the U-5 with Bernard and the U-7 with Mike Allen— grabbed the two inside lanes before the start of the final heat. *Oh Boy! Oberto* had lane three. The U-5, the U-7 and the U-6 ran one-two-three down the first backstretch. *Formulaboats.com II* (U-7) finished lap one in first-place but was passed by *Formulaboats.com I* (U-5) and *Oh Boy! Oberto*.

Formula I's lead over *Oberto* varied from one to one and a half roostertails. The winning speed by *Formula I* was 140.129 miles per hour to *Oberto*'s 139.299.

The victory was the first ever in the Unlimited Class by *Formula I* driver Bernard, who hailed from a multigenerational boat racing family. His stepfather, Terry Troxell, was a Gold Cup winner. Two of his uncles—Mark and Mike Weber—had driven Unlimiteds, and his grandfather, Ray Weber, had competed at Madison as far back as 1957 in a Limited hydroplane named *Mom's Worry*.

Oh Boy! Oberto/Miss Madison made it two National High Point Championships in a row in 2009. The team also won a second straight Tri-Cities Columbia Cup. There were some anxious moments on the last day of the season when Steve David flipped the boat in a preliminary heat at the UIM World Championship/Oryx Cup in Doha, Qatar. But *Oh Boy! Oberto* rebounded to finish second in the finale and claim the overall season title.

The road to the High Point Championship was a rocky one for the community-owned team. Mechanical gremlins at Seattle, the flip at Doha and a couple of penalty calls at Madison and Evansville took their toll. But

Left: Jean Theoret thanking the rescue diver who saved his life.

Below: Miss Bello's Pizza.

Oh Boy! Oberto hung tough and concluded the season with a 235-point edge over second-place *Miss E-Lam Plus.*

The most frightening mishap of 2009 occurred at Madison when Jean Theoret almost drowned when *Miss Bello's Pizza* flipped upside-down during a preliminary heat. Theoret was tangled in his five-point harness system until rescuers could pull him free. Jean spent the next few weeks in recovery but returned to competition a month later at Seattle.

Dave Villwock and *Miss E-Lam Plus* made the most of their return to full-time participation in Unlimited racing with a victory in the fifty-ninth annual Indiana Governor's Cup. *E-Lam* led out of the first turn in the winner-take-all final heat and throughout. Villwock averaged 138.054 miles per hour for the 12.5-mile distance, compared to 136.515 for J. Michael Kelly and *Graham Trucking*.

Jimmy King and the Allison-powered *Miss Chrysler Jeep* were drawing close to second-place Kelly but conked out one buoy marker short of the finish line. Steve David and *Oh Boy! Oberto/Miss Madison*, assigned to an unfavorable starting position, began in sixth place but worked their way up to take third.

Villwock's 2009 Madison victory made him the winningest driver in Indiana Governor's Cup history with eight victories since 1997. This put him one ahead of Bill Muncey (who had seven wins between 1960 and 1979) and Chip Hanauer (who had seven wins between 1984 and 1999).

The first decade of the new millennium ended on a happy note for fans of *Miss Madison* and the Madison Regatta. The Oberto-sponsored hydroplane took first place in the sixtieth annual running of the Indiana Governor's Cup with Steve David driving. This was the hometown favorite's first local victory since 2001 and the third since 1971. David pulled away to a commanding lead on lap two of the final heat and went on to average 139.485 for the 12.5-mile distance, compared to 135.963 for second-place J. Michael Kelly in *Graham Trucking* and 135.580 for third-place J.W. Myers in *Miss Peters & May*.

Oh Boy! Oberto/Miss Madison won its third straight National High Point Championship in 2010 and placed in the top three at all six races on the Unlimited tour. In addition to winning at home, the *Oberto* team was victorious in the Tri-Cities Columbia Cup and the Albert Lee Cup at Seattle. This marked the first time that a *Miss Madison* hydroplane had ever won three races in a given season.

For the first time since 2004, the Madison Regatta had a title sponsor, Lucas Oil, in 2010. This new arrangement was enthusiastically received by all concerned, with many references to a long and successful relationship in the years ahead.

Here's to the next hundred years of Unlimited hydroplane racing in Madison, Indiana!

A TIDAL WAVE OF DRAMA

The most dramatic series finish in history.

That's what people are saying about the 2009 Oryx Cup/UIM World Championship Race in Doha, Qatar. In the words of H1 Unlimited Chairman Sam Cole, "I can not remember any championship in the sport's history where so many factors came into play during the final three hours of the event."

Driver Steve David and the community-owned *Oh Boy! Oberto/Miss Madison* (U-1) seemed to be in a good position to repeat as Season High Point Champion. The U-1 had a first and two seconds in the first three preliminary heats and possessed a comfortable lead in National Points.

That lead evaporated, however, to almost nothing when the U-1 flipped and received no points in preliminary heat 4-A. The flip also relegated the U-1 to a most unfavorable position on the racecourse for the final heat in lane five.

And yet, when the roostertails subsided after the final heat, *Oh Boy! Oberto* had second place in the heat and first place in Season Points by a razor-thin margin.

According to H1 Unlimited vice-chairman Ken Muscatel, "*Oberto* was deserving and very lucky but was no more deserving that day than anyone else. And some of the challenges it had to overcome were self-inflicted. In the end, it worked out well for them and resulted in perhaps the most dramatic end to a race season in history."

When the North American phase of the 2009 H1 Unlimited tour concluded in August at Evansville, Indiana, three teams were "in the hunt" for the Season High Point Championship, which would be decided in November at Doha. These were *Oberto, Formulaboats.com* (U-5) with Jeff Bernard and *Miss E-Lam Plus* (U-16) with Dave Villwock.

Boat racing is one of the world's most unpredictable sports. There are so many factors, so many possible scenarios. On any given day, it could be anybody's boat race.

The 2009 Doha race marked the international debut of the H1 Unlimited Series. Races had previously been run in the United States, Canada and Mexico, but never in the Middle East. In the past, other forms of motor sports had made their presence felt in Qatar, but the thousands of spectators lining Doha Bay could not have asked for a more eloquent introduction to "Water Racing's Greatest Show." In heat after heat, the competition among the Unlimited hydroplanes was simply superb.

A disqualification at Evansville had cost the *Oh Boy! Oberto* dearly with the forfeiture of 550 points. *Miss E-Lam Plus* had likewise experienced difficulty—and lost points—on the North American circuit when it flipped at Evansville and suffered significant engine problems at the Tri-Cities, Washington.

Ten boats made the trans-Atlantic trek to Qatar. These included such highly regarded teams as *Graham Trucking* (U-7) with J. Michael Kelly, *Miss Peters & May* (U-37) with Jean Theoret and *Our Gang Racing* (U-17) with Nate Brown.

U-1 pilot Steve David knew that he faced an uphill fight to retain the High Point Championship. "Every race has an overall plan," he insisted, "which is accomplished through specific objectives, not unlike strategic planning in business.

> *We did not have an overwhelming lead coming into Doha. Nonetheless, if a couple of scenarios went our way, we would still be in good shape. That all began to come together when we drew the U-5 in heat 1-B. While the U-16 is always a threat, it was the U-5 that was closest to us in points. We were confident that we could beat the U-5 but we needed to draw him to do so. (At Evansville, he had escaped both the U-16 and us and we knew that was a possibility.)*

After the first three rounds of preliminaries, the U-16 had 1,200 accumulated heat points, compared to 1,000 for the U-1, 925 for the U-5 and 850 for the U-7. The U-1, nevertheless, led by 331 points for the season.

According to David, "In the fourth heat, all we had to do was beat the U-7 and we would have had the points locked in going into the final. We had beaten the U-7 in a prior heat and were confident that we could win against the U-7 from lane two.

"Then, the blow-over..."

While battling with the U-7 in heat 4-A, the U-1 became airborne and did a complete backward somersault. The blow-over was eerily reminiscent of the *Slo-mo-shun V* flip at Seattle in 1955.

As the U-1 lifted off the water, David's first thought was, "I just blew the National Championship! Secondly, I thought that this was going to hurt." Steve did in fact suffer a broken fibula cap in his right (throttle) leg, although this wasn't discovered until much later, after David had returned home to the United States.

> *Miracle of miracles, we landed right side up with minor damage. Now, it was a matter of "Will we be ready for the final and will we have a strong setup?" We were also concerned about what was going to happen points-wise with the U-5 and the U-16 in heat 4-B.*
>
> *Our team is nothing if not resourceful. They knew they could get the boat ready. They weren't so sure if I would be ready. Mike Hanson, the crew chief, asked me if I wanted to run the final out of genuine concern for both my physical and mental state. Well, there was no question, I was running the final. The team would give me a great boat again.*
>
> *However, we had pulled engine mount threads out of engine #1 and had to rely on a backup. It was a good engine but four miles per hour slower in overall lap speed than our top engine. That, coupled with a lane five draw, made the odds long again.*

While the U-1 team thrashed repairs, heat 4-B got underway. The outcome would prove crucial in the race for High Points. Both the U-16 and the U-5 jumped the gun and both had to run a penalty lap to be scored, while Jean Theoret and the U-37 inherited the 400 first-place heat points.

When it came time for the final heat of the season, just 156 points separated the U-1, the U-5 and the U-16. H1 Unlimited chairman Sam Cole commented, "I don't remember that happening before, with three different teams still in the race for the championship at the start of the final heat."

H1 Unlimited historian Fred Farley confirmed, saying, "It's never happened before when as little as 156 National Points separated three boats at the outset of the last heat of the season. At various times, two boats have gone down to the wire with a narrow points margin between them, but never three."

Hydroplane Racing in Small-Town Indiana

David's perfect landing following the flip kept him in the High Points race. But this meant that Bernard only had to finish two places ahead of him in the final to take the crown. With David starting in lane five and Bernard in lane two, that seemed very likely.

The starting gun for the final heat fired, and the U-16 led out of the first turn, followed closely by the U-5 with the U-1 trailing. Then, moments later, Bernard became airborne and did a barrel-roll, stopping the heat before the completion of lap one. Jeff escaped serious injury and managed to extricate himself from the cockpit, but the U-5 sustained major damage and was through for the day.

As things developed, the U-5 wasn't the only casualty in the first running of the final heat. Nate Brown's U-17 had encountered salt water and couldn't restart. The U-16 likewise got some salt water, but an engine change could not be made.

The withdrawal of the U-5 and the U-17 meant that the U-1 could move over from lane five to lane three with the U-16 in lane one and the U-7 in lane two. In order to retain the High Point Championship, the U-1 would have to finish at least second in the rerun of the final heat.

The shadows lengthened as the boats took to the water for the last time in 2009. H1 Unlimited vice-chairman Ken Muscatel was concerned about the setting sun. "If there had been any other delay," he said, "the race could not have been completed until the next day."

On the restart, Villwock and the U-16 moved to a commanding lead and an apparent victory that would give him the Oryx Cup and the Series Team Championship, while David and the U-1 trailed Kelly and the U-7 in third place.

According to Steve, "We were gaining on the U-7 and thought we could catch him. But then my radio person said what I thought was 'He blew over!' when in fact he said 'He's blowing flames!' in reference to the U-16.

"When I heard what I thought was a 'blow-over,' I immediately got out of the throttle. My radio person immediately got back on the radio and said, 'I meant losing an engine! Get on it!' We had lost probably half a straightaway on the U-7 at this point."

It appeared as though the *Oh Boy! Oberto/Miss Madison* was going to lose the championship on account of one position on the racecourse.

Then, on the final lap of the season, everything changed again. The turbine engine in Villwock's *Miss E-Lam Plus* (U-16) succumbed to salt water and slowed, allowing the U-7 to pass him for the lead and the win for the *Graham Trucking* sponsorship. The U-1 also passed the U-16 to take second in the Oryx Cup and secure the 2009 H1 Unlimited Series Championship for team *Oberto*. It was the first win in the Unlimited Class for J. Michael Kelly, who had qualified as an Unlimited driver in 2004.

Oh Boy! Oberto thus became the first non–*Miss Budweiser* team to win back-to-back season championships since *Atlas Van Lines* in 1983.

The point total for the season saw the U-1 with 7,970 points, the U-16 with 7,735, the U-5 with 7,564 and the U-7 with 6,689.

A jubilant Steve David proclaimed, "U-1 was our goal. Had we placed third in the final, I would have won the Drivers Title again, but this race and the season was about back-to-back U-1. We wanted to put an exclamation point on what this team could do running head-to-head against the U-16 all year long.

"One of the assets of a great team is having a bag full of options and strategies to draw upon at a moment's notice. Through scenario planning, considering multiple options and being prepared to implement any one of them in an instant, is the key to winning.

"You have to have the people who can create those scenarios, prepare those options, have the equipment at hand and know how to adjust instantly. Mike Hanson, Bob Hughes, Charlie Grooms, Larry Oberto and the team members have all of those qualities."

THE DRIVERS OF
MISS MADISON

O ver the past fifty years, a total of nineteen men have served as drivers of *Miss Madison*. Five of these—Buddy Byers, Jim McCormick, Ron Snyder, Mike Hanson and Steve David—managed to score at least one major victory for the team. Two drivers—Hanson and David—put in a decade or more of service; another driver—Morlan Visel—occupied the *Miss M* cockpit for but a single day with tragic consequences.

Marion Cooper was the original *Miss Madison* pilot and handled the community-owned craft during the 1961 and 1962 seasons. A boat racer since the 1930s, the Louisville resident piloted *Miss M* to its first victory—a secondary race at the 1961 World's Championship Seafair Regatta in Seattle. Visel, who replaced the retiring Cooper in 1963, was badly injured in a test run at the Gold Cup in Detroit when the boat struck floating debris and was destroyed. Visel survived the crash, but his death many years later was directly attributable to the injuries that he suffered while driving *Miss Madison*.

George "Buddy" Byers from Columbus, Ohio, was one of the top 7-Litre Limited drivers of the 1950s. He piloted *Miss Madison* to second place in National High Points in 1964 and third in 1965 and scored the first major victory for the *Miss M* team when he won the 1965 Dixie Cup at Guntersville, Alabama.

"Gentleman Jim" McCormick first served notice of his competitive prowess when he won the 266 Cubic Inch Class race at the 1964 Madison Regatta with *Miss Kathleen*. Two years later, McCormick was the rookie driver of *Miss Madison*. He went on to become the first *Miss M* pilot to win two races back to back—the 1971 APBA Gold Cup on home waters in Madison, Indiana, and the 1971 Tri-Cities (Washington) Atomic Cup.

Over the next few years, various drivers—Ed O'Halloran, Charlie Dunn, Tom Sheehy, Milner Irvin, Jerry Bangs, Jon Peddie and Andy Coker among them—took a turn in the *Miss Madison* cockpit. All represented the boat's thirteen thousand owners well with the equipment that was available but, in general, did not match the earlier successes of Buddy Byers and Jim McCormick.

An exception to the above summary is Ron Snyder, an on-again/off-again presence with the *Miss Madison* team between 1976 and 1988. Snyder posted fifteen top-three finishes. These included his 1983 victory in the Missouri Governor's Cup at Lake of the Ozarks. Ron achieved this triumph by making a perfect start in the winner-take-all final heat, while his much more affluent rivals—the *Atlas Van Lines* and the *Miss Budweiser*—made very poor starts and couldn't overtake the front-running Snyder.

Sooner or later, every Unlimited hydroplane team needs the services of a relief driver when the regular pilot is injured or unavailable. Three times in its history, the *Miss Madison* team has called upon veteran racer Jerry Hopp to fill in behind the wheel. Twice in 1986, Hopp substituted for Ron Snyder. In 2000, he relieved Charley Wiggins at Detroit when Jerry had about fifteen minutes notice before stepping into *Miss M*—a boat he had never driven. Hopp went on to take fifth in the Gold Cup.

Most people are surprised to see Mitch Evans included on the honor roll of *Miss Madison* drivers. The circumstances are unusual. In 1988, the new Ron Jones–designed *Miss Madison* was badly damaged in a blow-over accident at San Diego. The City of Madison leased Ed Cooper's *Risley's* (U-3) for a race the following weekend in Las Vegas. The *Risley's* became the *Miss Madison* for that one event. Evans, who regularly drove for the Cooper team, piloted the substitute *Miss M* to fifth place in the Silver Cup.

Mike Hanson made a one-time appearance with *Miss Madison* in 1988 at Seattle, where he was run over by another boat (*Miss Circus Circus*) while returning to the pits after one of the heat races. In 1989, Mike was promoted to full-time driver and hull specialist for the team. Hanson finished third in National High Points in 1989 and second in 1993 and won the Star Mart Cup in 1993 on San Diego's Mission Bay. Mike retired from the *Miss Madison* team after 1998 but returned in 2004 as crew chief.

Following the departure of Mike Hanson, Todd Yarling occupied the *Miss Madison* cockpit during the 1999 season. A resident of nearby Hanover, Indiana, Yarling flipped the boat at a race in Barrie, Ontario, but rebounded to take third place in the Virginia Is for Lovers Cup at Norfolk, Virginia.

A promising Limited competitor from Gadsden, Alabama, who had enjoyed considerable success in the Unlimited Light Class, Charley Wiggins had a painfully short tenure as driver of *Miss Madison*. Charley finished sixth in the 2000 Madison Regatta, but after suffering injuries at both Evansville and Detroit, he retired from racing.

Following the retirement of Charley Wiggins in mid-season 2000, veteran Unlimited competitor Nate Brown was hired by the *Miss Madison* team to drive at the three western races. Under the sponsorship of Oh Boy! Oberto, Brown qualified for all three final heats. He finished third at the Tri-Cities, fourth at Seattle and third at San Diego.

The most victorious *Miss Madison* driver of them all, Steve David joined the team in 2001. As of 2010, he has nine race wins with sponsor Oh Boy! Oberto. These include two victories (in 2001 and 2010) at the Madison Regatta. Steve guided the team to the National High Point Championship in 2008, 2009 and 2010. He himself was High Point Driver in 2005, 2006, 2008, 2009 and 2010. In 2010, he became the first *Miss Madison* driver to win three races in a given season. These were at Madison, the Tri-Cities and Seattle.

Marion Cooper—1961, 1962

Morlan Visel—1963

Buddy Byers—1963, 1964, 1965

Jim McCormick—1966, 1969, 1970, 1971

Ed O'Halloran—1967, 1968

Charlie Dunn—1972, 1973

Tom Sheehy—1973, 1982

Milner Irvin—1974, 1978, 1979, 1980, 1981, 1984

Jerry Bangs—1975

Ron Snyder—1976, 1982, 1983, 1984, 1986, 1987, 1988

Jon Peddie—1977, 1978

Hydroplane Racing in Small-Town Indiana

Andy Coker—1985, 1986

Jerry Hopp—1986, 2000

Mike Hanson—1988, 1989, 1990, 1991, 1992, 1993, 1994, 1995, 1996, 1997, 1998

Mitch Evans—1988

Todd Yarling—1999

Charley Wiggins—2000

Nate Brown—2000

Steve David—2001, 2002, 2003, 2004, 2005, 2006, 2007, 2008, 2009, 2010

THE MARION COOPER STORY

M arion Cooper will always be remembered as being the first in a distinguished line of *Miss Madison* drivers over the past five decades. A boat racer since the 1930s, Cooper piloted the community-owned craft during the 1961 and 1962 seasons.

Following his retirement from competition, Marion continued his association with the *Miss Madison* team. He was the one who would "break in" the new drivers. Cooper would take the boat out for a test run and check the systems. Then, he would turn the wheel over to the new man. He did this in 1963 with George "Buddy" Byers and in 1966 with Jim McCormick.

For most of his adult life, Marion was general manager of Louisville Motors in Louisville, Kentucky, where he applied the same no-nonsense approach to business as he did with racing. One of his employees was Jim Noonan, who served as a crew member on Cooper's Limited boats. Noonan eventually became an APBA referee. Noonan's sons, Mike and Billy, also became referees.

During the mid-1950s, Marion was briefly involved with several Unlimited teams. As a back-up driver for owner Stan Sayres, Cooper test-drove both *Slo-mo-shun IV* and *Slo-mo-shun V*. And on the recommendation of his friend Joe Taggart, Marion drove Austin Snell's *Miss Rocket* in the 1957 Gold Cup at Seattle.

The *Miss Madison* was a very low-budget operation in the early days. Everyone from crew chief Graham Heath on down was a volunteer. Cooper had to pay his own way to the races.

In a 1973 interview with APBA Unlimited historian Fred Farley, Marion recalled, "I had often driven for Neal Cahall and Dick Cox in the 225s and 266s. They were involved in the *Miss Madison* organization when Sam DuPont gave them the first boat. They called me and wanted to know if I would drive it and, of course, I was happy to do so.

> *During that first year, they didn't have another stock Allison engine. So, the same engine was run the entire season. We tried to hold the rpms down to around 4000 to 4100. If it went above that, it was only for a short time. We didn't figure it would run very long above that.*
>
> *At the end of the season, since the Madison Regatta was the last race, the organization said I could let it go. So, I did and took fourth in an eleven-boat field.*

That was the start of a fifty-year competitive tradition for the City of Madison that continues to the present day. No other Unlimited hydroplane team in history can match the *Miss Madison* in the number of consecutive years of participation.

During his tenure as the original *Miss Madison* driver, Marion also took fifth in both the 1961 Detroit Memorial Regatta and the 1961 President's Cup, sixth in the 1962 Gold Cup, fourth in the 1962 Spirit of Detroit Trophy and third in the 1962 Indiana Governor's Cup. Cooper finished every heat that he started with the *Miss Madison* and scored points in all but two.

Cooper's first competitive performance behind the wheel of a race boat occurred in 1937 at Cincinnati, Ohio, with the 510 Cubic Inch Class *Hermes*, a craft in which he had served an apprenticeship as riding mechanic for several years.

> *I rode with my brother, George Cooper, back in the days when there were two-man boats. Turley Carman and George Davis had built the boat, which used an OX-5 aircraft engine. The rocker arms were on the outside with no cover over them. I think the top rpm on the engine was about 1400. It turned through a gear box and got up to speeds of 60 to 65 miles an hour—maybe 70.*
>
> *Back in the pre–World War II days, you didn't have such things as fuel pumps. You had to have someone to operate the hand pressure pump.*

The riding mechanic had to watch the gauge and keep the right amount of pressure in the fuel tank to keep from flooding the thing. He had to keep the pressure up to as much as five pounds and not over six. That went on for years because the pumps they had up to that time wouldn't supply enough fuel.

For instance, the Hisso-powered Mercury that I had, at one time, used eight dual Stromberg carburetors and it took a lot of fuel to supply those things. Of course, in one sense of the word, it was a dangerous proposition running pressure on the tank because it resulted in fires occasionally, on account of the pressure on the tank would sometimes break loose. But we were always able to put it out before it got too bad.

Cooper's next boat was the *Hermes III*, a highly successful 725 Cubic Inch Class step hydroplane, which campaigned during 1937 and 1938 with a V-8 Hispano-Suiza (Hisso) engine.

With George Davis alongside in the mechanic's seat, Marion won the 725 Class event at the 1937 Gold Cup Regatta in Detroit and posted a first heat average speed of 54.800 miles per hour over contenders such as Bill Cantrell in *Why Worry*, Jim Anderson in *Warnie* and Cam Fischer in *Miss Cincinnati Jr.*

"In that race," Marion recalled, "Jim Vetter in *Miss Trailmobile* ran over the top of the *Warnie*, fell on our boat, and knocked out our freeboard. But we went on and finished the race anyway. Although, they had to pull us out pretty quick because it would have sunk."

Painted black and yellow with orange checkers on the foredeck, *Hermes III* measured 22½ feet by 5½ feet with a sharp curving bow and a deep notch across the bottom amidships and was equipped with a three-bladed brass propeller that turned around 3600 rpm for every 2400 revolutions of the Hisso power plant.

In later years, it was renamed *Pin Brain IV* by another owner but not before the team of Cooper, Davis and *Hermes III* triumphed in the Calvert Trophy at Louisville and the 725 Class contest at Evansville, Indiana, during the summer of 1938.

Cooper's first experience with a sponson-type rig was in the *Mercury*, which, for two hours, was the fastest boat in the world in its category with a ninety-eight-mile-an-hour straightaway clocking at the 1940 President's Cup Regatta in Washington, D.C., before Cantrell did ninety-nine with *Why Worry*.

We had higher compression on the Mercury than on Hermes III. We also had a little better carburetion on it. It was real wide and most of the sponsors were built underneath. Only about four or five inches of the sponsons stuck out from the sides. Mercury was built similar to a Ventnor, except that the Ventnor hulls had the sponsons all to the outside. It was pretty close to the design of a two-point hull, which nobody knew much about then.

In fact, it kept trying to run on the two points a lot of times and we kept moving the weight back to try to keep the back end down, which was the wrong thing to do. If we had kept the weight forward, it probably would have run on two points.

Before World War II lowered the curtain on the 725 Class and Cooper's participation in it, Marion, together with riding mechanic Charlie Schott, pushed *Mercury* to victory at the 1940 Evansville Jaycees Regatta and the 1942 Emil Auerbach Memorial Trophy Race on Biscayne Bay, which carried with it the 725 Class National Championship.

His major competition during those years was Cantrell's *Why Worry*. Between the two of them, Bill and Marion accounted for most of the major trophies on the Mississippi Valley Power Boat Association (MVPBA) circuit.

Mercury and *Why Worry* also made their presences felt in races against the generally more expensive and more exotic-looking APBA Gold Cup Class contenders. The 725 Class circuit usually consisted of from eight to ten races, wherein the boats ran clockwise because their engines turned that way. Flag starts without any blackout clock were also the rule.

After World War II, the 725 Class and the Gold Cup Class combined and changed over to the Unlimited Class. According to Cooper, "The 725s rode rougher than your Unlimiteds do today. Of course, an Unlimited is about as easy riding a boat of them all. Although, when you get a jolt in an Unlimited, it's a good one."

After the war, Marion saw action primarily in the 225, 266 and 7-Litre Classes. He owned nine Limited hulls and built three of them himself. In 1946, he won the 225 Class National Championship Race with *Hornet* and, in 1955, set a world competition heat record of 81.008 with the 7-Litre Class *Hornet*.

He won the 225 Class race at the 1949 Madison Regatta and the 1951 Indiana Governor's Cup at Madison with *Hornet*. In 1960, while driving *Louisville Kid*, Cooper finished second to Buddy Byers in the 7-Litre Class World Championship Race that was run at Madison. He was also a silent partner in *It's a Wonder*, a former 725 Class rig, owned and driven by George Davis.

Few drivers have had longer career spans where participation in the APBA Gold Cup is concerned. (His first ride in the Gold Cup was the 1939 event at Detroit with *Mercury*, and his last was the 1962 affair at Seattle with *Miss Madison*.) Marion was also a three-time winning chauffeur of the Calvert Trophy, the premier award at the annual Marine Derby Regatta in Louisville, with victories in 1938 with *Hermes III* and in 1954 and 1955 with *Hornet*. He also captured the 1966 Calvert Trophy as owner of *Louisville Kid* with driver Bill Cousins.

Cooper's most memorable race with *Miss Madison* occurred on the warm and sunny afternoon of August 5, 1961, during the Seafair Regatta on Lake Washington. Three races of 45 miles in length were run that day for fast, middle and slow qualifiers. *Miss M* triumphed in the intermediate race for the Seattle Trophy with heat speeds of 99.046, 98.937 and 100.074. Each heat was five laps around a 3-mile course.

In the First Heat, I got up to the starting line a little too early and had to back off. By the time I got on it again, the others had all gone by me. I stayed back there in all that rough water until about the last lap when I went by two of the three boats ahead of me on the outside and took second-place points.

In the next two heats, I got good starts and won both of them. Although, in the second heat, the exhaust stack broke off on the right side and was firing into the hull, which finally started to blaze. Then a three-quarter-inch water plug on the right bank blew out. And the water from that plug started hitting and putting the fire out. The resulting steam was flying about seven or eight feet in the air. And I think everybody thought that the engine was cooking. But it wasn't. I watched the temperature gauge, but the water from that plug kept the fire down until we finished. Of course, for the final heat, they put another exhaust stack on and another plug in it, and everything was all right again.

The memory of that race is especially fond, due to the enormous crowd and because the race in Seattle was a big deal—more so than anyplace else in the country.

In his later years, Cooper remained a familiar and popular boat racing figure. He always attended the annual Madison Regatta, accompanied by his wife, Mildred, and his old friend and partner from the 725 Class days, George Davis.

In counseling new drivers just starting out, Cooper believed that

if a rookie can get into an Unlimited, then that's the thing to do. He could learn to drive in that just as easy as he could by starting in a Limited. That's because they drive entirely different. Of course, that doesn't happen very often, but it does happen occasionally. And I'd say he would be as good a driver as one who started small and then worked his way up.

The two hard points about driving an Unlimited are in going way back at the start and in keeping the transom up going around the turns. If you let it drop, you may as well forget about it on account of the three-to-one gear ratio.

When asked about the changes that he had observed in the sport since his departure from it, Marion was one of the first to recognize the potential of the horizontal stabilizer wing that the Ron Jones–designed *Pay 'n Pak* introduced to good effect in 1973: "You'll see more of those lift-wings stuck on the back ends of more boats. They're a big help in getting around a corner."

On the subject of the great drivers of the past and present, Marion felt it was "pretty much of a draw. Bill Cantrell was rough. But of the new ones, I would just as soon risk Dean Chenoweth with a boat as any at all."

Marion Cooper passed away on February 21, 1986, while on a vacation to Florida. He was eighty-two. Cooper's longtime friend and fellow competitor, Bill Cantrell, offered the following eulogy: "He was quite a guy! Marion was congenial, likeable, and he was always willing to help out if another guy needed help on his boat. He was a hard driver—a good driver!"

THE BUDDY BYERS STORY

The distinction of winning the first major race in the fifty-year history of the community-owned *Miss Madison* belongs to George "Buddy" Byers of Columbus, Ohio. The victory in question was the 1965 Dixie Cup at Guntersville, Alabama. Byers and *Miss Madison* entered the final heat on Guntersville Lake with two second-place finishes in the preliminary action. Sprinting toward the starting line, Buddy realized that he and the other drivers were too early and in danger of "jumping the gun." Byers eased off on the throttle and wisely resisted the impulse to follow when the rest of the field thundered past him.

Sure enough, front-runners *Miss U.S. 5*, *Notre Dame* and *Tahoe Miss* all crossed prematurely and incurred a one-lap penalty. Buddy backpedaled to a legal start, cruised to an easy victory and wound up with 1,000 accumulated points, 73 more than the second-place finisher, *Mariner Too*, driven by Warner Gardner. This was in the days when the winner of an Unlimited hydroplane race was determined on total point accumulation rather than by the order of finish in the final heat.

Byers was one of the top 7-Litre Class Limited Inboard drivers of the 1950s and early sixties. Piloting boats named *Chrysler Queen* and *Miss Desoto*, he won two Nationals and six High Point Championships. Moreover, Byers set a world 7-Litre Class straightaway record of 151.271 miles per hour in 1958.

All ten of the 7-Litre boats that he owned were custom-built for him by the highly regarded Henry Lauterbach.

Not until late in his career did Buddy advance to the Unlimited ranks. He made his initial appearance in the cockpit of *Miss M* at the 1963 Madison Regatta, where he placed fifth in the Indiana Governor's Cup.

Byers had a big year in 1964. He gave an extremely consistent performance that allowed him to finish second in the National Point Standings. And although he didn't win a race, Buddy had *Miss Madison* running better than in its initial season as *Nitrogen Too* in 1960.

And everywhere he competed, *Miss M* served as the best ambassador of goodwill that the tiny midwestern town had ever had. Indeed, the city of Madison, Indiana, became a household word from coast to coast, thanks to the fast-moving U-6, its intrepid driver, Buddy Byers, and its masterful crew chief, Graham Heath.

For 1966, Buddy was contracted to drive Bill Harrah's casino-sponsored *Tahoe Miss*, a very competitive craft that had won two races in 1965 with Chuck Thompson as driver. With the best equipment money could buy, Byers was expected to be a formidable presence in the season ahead. But that never came to pass. While driving in a 7-Litre race at Miami Marine Stadium, Buddy was seriously injured and lost partial use of his right arm. In the twinkling of an eye, his racing career was over.

But instead of retiring to his Columbus-based truck and auto agencies, Byers embarked on a new career as an Unlimited official. For several years, he served as Unlimited Drivers' representative. And in 1970, he succeeded his friend J. Lee Schoenith as the APBA Unlimited commissioner, a position that he was to occupy for eleven years.

With Buddy as commissioner, the sport enjoyed considerable progress. In 1972, the Jim Hendrick Powerboat Radio Network was established. The minimum prize money package per race increased from $25,000 to $57,500. And perhaps most significantly of all, the door was opened in 1973 for the introduction of turbine power in the Unlimited Class, as an answer to the ever-dwindling supply of World War II aircraft power sources.

After stepping down as commissioner, Byers returned to his first love—driving a race boat. At the 1997 APBA Gold Cup, Buddy made a triumphant return, piloting the restored 7-Litre *Chrysler Queen* in an exhibition run on the Detroit River.

THE JIM McCORMICK STORY

In 1971, the community-owned *Miss Madison* and driver Jim McCormick made their claim to immortality with an exciting triumph before 110,000 partisan fans on the Ohio River at Madison, Indiana. This was a victory for the amateur, the common man, a win that everyone could claim as his own.

Miss Madison's victory was historic on several counts. Not since the 1965 Dixie Cup at Guntersville, Alabama, with Buddy Byers driving had the sun-bleached *Miss M* scored a victory. It was pilot McCormick's first win in the Unlimited Class. *Miss Madison* was built in 1959 and first entered competition in 1960 (as *Nitrogen Too*), thereby making it the only Unlimited hydroplane to win a Gold Cup eleven years after its competition debut.

The 1971 event also marked the only time that a community-owned boat had ever won racing's most coveted prize. Not since *Tahoe Miss* in 1966 had the Gold Cup race winner used Allison—rather than Rolls-Royce Merlin—aircraft power. *Miss Madison* also represented the end of an era. It was the last Unlimited hydroplane with the old-style rear-cockpit/forward-engine/shovel-nosed bow configuration to achieve victory.

To prove that the hometown performance was anything but a fluke, *Miss Madison* captured first-place honors in the Tri-Cities Atomic Cup three weeks later on the Columbia River at Kennewick, Washington.

Prior to being tapped for the *Miss Madison* assignment, Jim McCormick was an obscure Midwest Limited inboard participant. Jim nevertheless served notice of his competitive prowess when he won the 266 Cubic Inch Class race at the 1964 Madison Regatta with *Miss Kathleen*.

An air conditioning contractor from Owensboro, Kentucky, Jim's first appearance in an Unlimited hydroplane cockpit was at the 1966 Tampa Suncoast Cup, where he steered *Miss Madison* (U-6) to an overall third-place finish with a victory in the first heat. During 1966, he completed all but two of the nineteen heats in which he started with *Miss M* and finished eighth in a field of twenty-three drivers in the National High Point Standings.

After starting the 1967 season with *Notre Dame*, he replaced owner Bob Fendler in the cockpit of *Wayfarers Club Lady* and went on to place third in a field of twenty-two drivers in the National Standings. While driving the *Wayfarer*, he set the fastest qualifying marks at each of the Atomic Cup, Gold Cup and British Columbia Cup races with speeds of 110.837, 118.507 and 112.782—the latter a world record for a 2.5-mile course.

In 1968, McCormick divided his time between *Atlas Van Lines* (U-35) and *Harrah's Club* (U-3). His best finish was a third at the Arizona Governor's Cup with *Harrah's Club*. While driving the U-3, he was the only driver to defeat National Champions Billy Schumacher and *Miss Bardahl* three times in heat competition—twice at Seattle and once at Phoenix.

In 1969, Jim returned to *Miss Madison*, which he drove in four eastern races and placed third in the Madison Regatta. For the western tour, he handled *Atlas Van Lines* (U-19)—the former *Wayfarers Club Lady*—and posted the highest finish of his career thus far, a second-place at the Seattle Seafair Regatta.

It is interesting to note that twice in his career, McCormick was called upon to bail out a major team that had started the season with a highly touted rookie driver who ultimately couldn't make the competitive grade. In 1968, he replaced Burnett Bartley in *Harrah's Club*, and in 1969, he succeeded Earl Wham in *Atlas Van Lines*. Both Bartley and Wham came to the Unlimited ranks with impressive credentials from the Limiteds. But as Unlimited drivers, they were total nonentities. Enter Jim McCormick. All of a sudden, the boats were contenders with significant increases in heat speeds.

For the next two seasons, Jim drove exclusively for *Miss Madison*, although he almost missed the 1970 campaign entirely. *Miss Madison* was involved in a highway accident in Georgia while en route to the first race of the season in Tampa, Florida. Pulled off the circuit, the stricken craft underwent repairs by original builder Les Staudacher. In retrospect, the mishap was probably a blessing. Staudacher used the occasion to go through the entire hull and fix several things in addition to the highway accident damage that might otherwise have gone unnoticed.

The end result was an improved contender when *Miss M* returned to action a month later. Had the National Championship been determined that year solely on the results of the five races that the *Miss Madison* did enter, discounting the three that it missed, the team would have finished fourth instead of sixth.

Jim and *Miss M* defeated the highly regarded Tommy "Tucker" Fults and *Pay 'n Pak's 'Lil Buzzard* in heat 1-B at Madison, which was a surprise. The U-6 also showed a lot of class—and a definite increase in speed—when it and McCormick trounced the favored Bill Muncey and *Myr Sheet Metal* in both heats 1-C and 3-A of the season-concluding San Diego Gold Cup.

At year's end, *Miss Madison* was running the best of its long career and giving the better-than-average performance that was expected of it. It could make the front-runners work for it and could run with them on occasion. But the general consensus at the outset of 1971 was that only a newer hull and more power would put the U-6 team in the winner's circle. Nevertheless, the *Miss Madison* organization decided to stay with their eleven—going on twelve—year-old craft for one more season.

The 1971 campaign started with a new race, the Champion Spark Plug Regatta, on Biscayne Bay at Miami Marine Stadium. *Miss M* was leading in both of its preliminary heats but was forced to drop back on account of a fuel mixture problem in section 1-A and a faulty supercharger in 2-B. Not to be denied a spot in the finale, the volunteer crew members proved their mettle by performing a complete engine change in less than thirty minutes. Pilot McCormick then proceeded to take second spot in both the third heat and the overall standings behind Dean Chenoweth and the *Miss Budweiser*.

Miss Madison continued in the Champion Regatta a resurgence that had begun in the last race of 1970. No longer was the U-6 thought of as a slightly better-than-average boat that was merely along for the ride. The *Miss M* was now regarded as a viable contender. However, the team was still short on money and horsepower, and most people still refused to take the community-owned boat seriously.

Moving on to the President's Cup contest on the Potomac River, *Miss Madison* won its first two heats convincingly. It defeated the likes of Billy Schumacher in *Pride of Pay 'n Pak*, Leif Borgersen in *Hallmark Homes* and Billy Sterett Jr. in *Notre Dame*, each of which had a millionaire owner and used the more powerful Rolls-Royce Merlin engine.

Prior to the finale, *Miss M* and Jim McCormick were not an illogical choice to win the race, based upon their strong showing in the preliminary action. Charging into the first turn of the championship heat, however, the

U-6 was hosed down by the roostertails of *Hallmark Homes* and the eventual winner, *Atlas Van Lines I*, handled by Bill Muncey. McCormick managed to restart and take a disappointing fourth behind *Hallmark*, *Atlas I* and *Miss Budweiser*, although he managed to overtake and outrun *Pride of Pay 'n Pak* by a wide margin.

The *Miss Madison* team won the overall second-place President's Cup trophy for 1971 and had the satisfaction of running both the fastest fifteen-mile heat and the swiftest forty-five-mile race of the contest. But driver McCormick was bitterly discouraged. He had missed victory by a scant thirty-one points and was beginning to wonder if winning a race wasn't perhaps an impossible dream.

In the Kentucky Governor's Cup at Owensboro, *Miss M* did not improve on its two previous performances, taking an overall third behind *Atlas Van Lines I* and *Pride of Pay 'n Pak*. The U-6 challenged *Miss Budweiser* for the lead in heat two, but otherwise its performance was undistinguished.

At the Horace E. Dodge Cup in Detroit, *Miss Madison* ran head to head with Terry Sterett and *Atlas Van Lines II* (the former *Myr Sheet Metal*) in the first heat, despite rough water. On the last lap, Sterett moved ahead of McCormick and maintained this advantage to win by three boat lengths.

In the second heat, *Miss M* broke down and recorded its first DNF (did not finish) of the year. Consequently, the U-6 was ineligible for the finale. Still, *Miss Madison* was running the best of its almost ended career.

The Thunderboat trail now led to Madison, Indiana, which was steeped in a competitive tradition that dated back nearly six decades. For the first time since 1951, the Indiana Governor's Cup shared the spotlight with the APBA Gold Cup, powerboating's crown jewel, which had never before in modern times been run in so small a town as Madison. Due to a technicality and a misunderstanding, the $30,000 bid for the race by the sponsoring Madison Regatta, Inc., was the only one submitted in time to the Gold Cup Contest Board.

For ten years, the volunteer *Miss Madison* mechanical crew had tried to win the hometown race, without success. They faced an uphill fight in 1971, and they knew it. In the first four races of the season, *Miss Budweiser* and *Atlas Van Lines I* had both scored two solid victories apiece. *Atlas Van Lines II*, a five-race winner in 1969–70, was likewise a formidable contender. (Having been its team's number one entry during the three previous years, the *II*'s performance had suffered little in its secondary role with Terry Sterett in the cockpit.)

Also not to be overlooked in the pre-race figuring at the Madison Gold Cup were the *Hallmark Homes*, the *Notre Dame* and the *Pride of Pay 'n Pak*.

Hallmark was having a difficult season but nevertheless had championship credentials, being the former 1967–68 Gold Cup and National High Point–winning *Miss Bardahl*. *Notre Dame*, a virtual copy of *Hallmark Homes*, had a reputation as being a fast competitive boat, although it had never won a race. *Pay 'n Pak* was likewise having an uneven 1971 campaign. The *Pak* sported a radical new design. It was wider, flatter, less box-shaped, had a pickle-forked bow configuration and had performed admirably on occasion. The craft had experienced a disastrous 1970 season, but there were a few who staunchly believed that if *Pride of Pay 'n Pak* ever had the "bugs" ironed out of it, it would revolutionize the sport and render obsolete all of the top contenders of the previous twenty years.

Several days before the race, Jim McCormick placed a crucial telephone call to Reno, Nevada. He requested and obtained the services of two of the finest Allison engine specialists in the sport—Harry Volpi and Everett Adams of the defunct *Harrah's Club* racing team—who flew to Madison and worked in the pits alongside U-6 regulars Tony Steinhardt, Bob Humphrey, Dave Stewart, Keith Hand and Russ Willey. Volpi and Adams are credited with perfecting the *Miss Madison*'s water-alcohol injection system.

Race day, July 4, 1971, dawned bright and warm with ten qualified boats prepared to do competitive battle. A crowd of 110,000 fans literally choked the small midwestern town of 13,000. The river conditions were good, but *Miss M* was down to its last engine, having blown the other in trials. This put the U-6 people at a distinct disadvantage because, at that time, the Gold Cup Race consisted of four fifteen-mile heats instead of the usual three.

The race was less than thirty seconds old when *Hallmark Homes* disintegrated in a geyser of spray and sank in the first turn of heat 1-A, after encountering the roostertail of *Atlas Van Lines I*. *Hallmark* pilot Leif Borgersen escaped injury, but his boat was totaled.

Miss Madison was drawn into heat 1-B along with *Towne Club*, *Miss Timex*, the *Smoother Mover* and *Atlas Van Lines II*. During the warm-up period, *Smoother Mover* joined *Hallmark Homes* at the bottom of the river when its supercharger blew and punched a hole in the *Mover*'s underside.

Miss M had the lead at the end of lap one but was then passed by *Atlas II*. On lap three, the Fred Alter–chauffeured *Towne Club* began to challenge *Miss Madison* for second place. McCormick and Alter seesawed back and forth for several laps and brought the crowd to its feet. *Miss M* managed to outrun the *Towne Club* and hang on for second-place points behind the front-running *Atlas II*.

For the second round of preliminaries, *Miss Madison* matched skills with *Miss Budweiser*, *Notre Dame* and *Atlas I* in heat 2-B. Bill Muncey reached the first turn first with *Atlas I*, followed by *Miss M. Budweiser* and *Notre Dame* were both watered down by Muncey's roostertail, causing both to go dead in the water. *Atlas I* widened its lead over the field down the first backstretch and in the ensuing laps, while *Miss Madison* settled into a safe second. *Miss Budweiser* immediately restarted to follow *Miss M* around the course in third place. *Notre Dame* also managed to restart but only after being lapped by the field.

At the end of fifteen miles, Muncey and *Atlas I* received the green flag instead of the checkered flag, indicating a one-lap penalty for a foul against *Miss Budweiser* and *Notre Dame* in the first turn for violation of the overlap rule. This moved *Miss Madison* from second to first position in the corrected order of finish. *Miss Budweiser* was given second place, and *Atlas I* wound up officially in third after running seven laps before *Notre Dame* could finish six.

After another random draw, *Miss M* found itself in heat 3-B along with *Atlas II*, *Notre Dame* and *Pride of Pay 'n Pak*. As Bill Muncey was preparing to drive *Atlas I* before Heat 3-A, he received word that Referee Bill Newton had put him on probation for the next three races of the season. The probation had resulted not only from the foul against the field in heat 2-B but also from the cumulative effect of similar infractions by Muncey in 1970 at Seattle and San Diego. The consequence of the probation was that any further violations by Muncey would result in an indefinite suspension from racing.

Unperturbed, Muncey made a good start in heat 3-A and was chasing Dean Chenoweth and *Miss Budweiser* down the first backstretch when *Atlas I* sheared off its right sponson and started taking on water. Bill frantically tried to steer his wounded craft toward the bank on the Kentucky side of the river but was unable to do so. *Atlas Van Lines I* rolled over on its side about one hundred feet from shore and slipped beneath the surface, forcing Muncey to abandon ship. Now, three boats rested at the bottom of the Ohio.

Terry Sterett and *Atlas II* entered the first turn of heat 3-B in the lead and stayed there, but *Miss Madison* kept nipping at their heels. *Pride of Pay 'n Pak*, running in third, tried to overtake *Miss M*, but the U-6 pulled away to maintain second position. On the last lap, *Miss Madison* came on hard to finish only two seconds behind *Atlas II* and four seconds ahead of *Pay 'n Pak*.

After three grueling sets of elimination heats, the five qualifiers for the final go-around comprised *Atlas II* with 1,100 accumulated points, *Miss Madison* with 1,000 points, *Pride of Pay 'n Pak* with 869, *Towne Club* with 750 and *Miss Budweiser* with 700.

As the sun started to set on that historic July 4, the race for the Gold Cup and the Governor's Cup boiled down to *Atlas Van Lines II* and *Miss Madison*. *Miss M* had to make up a deficit of 100 points in order to win the championship. To do this, the U-6 would have to finish first in the final fifteen-mile moment of truth. This appeared rather unlikely since the combination of Terry Sterett and *Atlas II* had bested the team of Jim McCormick and *Miss Madison* in each of their four previous match-ups that season, twice on the Ohio River and twice the previous weekend on the Detroit River.

As the field took to the water for the last time, some of the hometown fans hung on to the hope that perhaps *Atlas II* would fail to start and thereby allow the local favorite to win the big race by default. But that was not to be. As McCormick wheeled *Miss M* out onto the 2.5-mile course, there was Sterett, starting up and pulling out of the pit area right behind him. Thus, as the final minutes and seconds ticked away, the die was cast. If McCormick hoped to achieve his first career victory on this day, he would have to earn it—the hard way.

Meanwhile, the ABC *Wide World of Sports* television crew members, who were there taping the race for a delayed national broadcast, decided among themselves that Terry Sterett was a shoo-in for the title. Accordingly, they set up their camera equipment in the *Atlas II*'s pit area in anticipation of interviewing the victorious Sterett when he returned to the dock.

All five finalists were on the course and running. Moments before the one-minute gun, *Miss Madison* was observed cruising down the front straightaway in front of the pit area. Then, abruptly, McCormick altered course, making a hard left turn into the infield. He sped across course, making a beeline for the entrance buoy of the upper corner. His strategy was obvious. McCormick wanted the inside lane to force the other boats to run a wider—and longer—course.

As the field charged underneath the Milton/Madison Bridge, four of the five boats were closely bunched with Fred Alter's *Towne Club* on the extreme outside, skirting the shoreline. *Miss Madison* had lane one; *Atlas Van Lines II* had lane two and was slightly in the lead when the starting gun fired.

Sprinting toward the first turn, *Pride of Pay 'n Pak* spun out. *Atlas II* made it into and out of the turn in front with *Miss Madison* close behind on the inside. As the field entered the first backstretch, the order was *Atlas, Madison, Budweiser, Pay 'n Pak* and *Towne Club*.

Then McCormick made his move. After having run a steady conservative race all day long, "Gentleman Jim" slammed the accelerator to the floor. The boat took off like a shot and thundered past Terry Sterett as if his rival had been tied to the dock.

The partisan crowd screamed in unison, "GO! GO! GO!" Even hardened veterans of racing were dumbfounded. An aging, underpowered, underfinanced museum piece was leading the race and leaving the rest of the field to wallow in its wake.

McCormick whipped *Miss M* around the upper turn expertly and sped under the bridge and back down the river to the start/finish line. It was one down and five laps to go. The *Atlas*, the *Budweiser* and the *Pay 'n Pak* were closely bunched at this point as they followed *Miss Madison* around the buoys.

The crowd was going absolutely wild. In lap two, McCormick increased his lead. And in lap three, he extended his advantage even more.

It dawned on the *Wide World of Sports* crew that an upset was in the making. Frantically, the ABC-TV technicians scrambled out of the *Atlas* pit area and hustled their camera gear over to the *Miss Madison*'s pits.

Out on the racecourse, Sterett had shaken free of *Budweiser* and *Pay 'n Pak* and was going all out after *Miss M*. He was fast on the straightaways, but not as fast as McCormick. The *Atlas* cornered well, but not as well as the U-6.

Miss Madison was running flawlessly, its twenty-six-year old Allison engine not missing a beat. Jim McCormick was driving the race of his life. Together, the boat and driver made an inspired combination. Bonnie McCormick, Jim's wife, who had averted her eyes during the first few laps, was now concentrating fully on the action, cheering her husband on at the top of her lungs.

Miss M received the green flag, indicating one more lap to the checkered flag and victory. By now, the community-owned craft had a decisive lead. Sterett was beaten, and he knew it. The *Atlas* pilot could only hope against hope that a mechanical problem or a driving error would slow the *Miss M* down.

But that didn't happen. McCormick made one last perfect turn. The *Miss M*'s roostertail kicked skyward. The boat streaked under the bridge, past Bennett's dock and over the finish line, adding a new chapter to American sports legend, as pandemonium broke loose on the shore.

Fire bells rang, automobile horns sounded and the spectators went out of their minds with delight. Everybody, it seemed, was a U-6 fan and, whether they lived there or not, a Madisonian. Even members of rival teams were applauding the outcome of this modern-day Horatio Alger story.

Miss Madison had beaten *Atlas Van Lines II* by 16.3 seconds in the final heat and was 4.2 seconds swifter for the overall sixty miles. McCormick and Sterett had tied with 1,400 points apiece in the four heats of racing. According to Unlimited Class rules, a point tie is broken by the order of finish in the last heat of the day. So, the U-6 won all the marbles. These included an engraved plate that would say *Miss Madison* to be added to the rows of gleaming testimonials to the conquests of Gar Wood, George Reis, Danny Foster, Stan Sayres, Bill Muncey and others.

It was the biggest day in the history of Madison, Indiana. It was Unlimited hydroplane racing at its best. And not since the *Slo-mo-shun* days in Seattle during the 1950s had such an outpouring of civic emotion occurred at a Gold Cup Race, with people celebrating in the streets until ten o'clock that night.

Deliriously happy *Miss Madison* crew members carried pilot McCormick on their shoulders to the judges' stand. Veteran boat racer George N. Davis, a mentor of McCormick's during Jim's 280 Class career, wept unashamedly at this, his protégé's moment of triumph.

After receiving the Gold Cup from 1946 winner Guy Lombardo and the Governor's Cup from Indiana Governor Edgar Whitcomb, a tired but happy McCormick explained his race strategy to the assembled legion of awe-struck media representatives: "We planned to take it easy in the early heats, and then let it all hang out in the finals."

McCormick was the first to give credit where credit was due. He quickly acknowledged that without the mechanical prowess of his volunteer pit crew, victory would have been impossible. "These guys have been working their hearts out getting ready for this. They deserve all the credit."

The *Miss Madison* crew received the Markt A. Lytle Sportsmanship Trophy at the Gold Cup Awards Banquet, where tribute was also paid to the two former *Harrah's Club* team members—Volpi and Adams—for their invaluable help in winning "the big one."

"Gentleman Jim" McCormick, who had achieved his "Impossible Dream," was the hero of the day, and he gratefully acknowledged the enthusiasm of the crowd. For several hours after the trophy presentation, McCormick, still in his driving suit, remained at the judges' stand, signing his name for one and all. "Let the people come," he said. "I'll sign autographs as long as I can write." It was the perfect ending to a perfect day.

As the spectators and participants drifted back to their own lives, one thought was uppermost in the minds of many: "Was it all a dream, or did today really happen?"

Yes, it did happen. And it happened again three weeks later on the Columbia River at the Tri-Cities, Washington. That's when *Miss Madison* driver McCormick and crew members Steinhardt, Stewart, Humphrey, Hand and Willey made the incredible seem commonplace. They won the sixth annual Atomic Cup Race and, in so doing, moved from second to first place in the National Season Points chase.

Entering the final heat in fourth place in regatta points with two second-place finishes, *Miss M* was again lightly regarded as a title threat. The boat's nitrous oxide system (which gives the craft an added burst of speed coming off the corners) had failed to function during the first two heats. In fact, the crew wasn't even certain if the engine was going to start for the finale. But, in McCormick's words, "We got it all together," and not a moment too soon.

Most attention centered on Billy Schumacher in the *Pride of Pay 'n Pak* and Bill Muncey in the now repaired *Atlas Van Lines I*, who led the field with only one hundred points separating them. The futuristic *Pay 'n Pak* looked especially formidable that day and seemed on the verge of coming into its own, although many experts were still siding with *Atlas I* to win due to that boat's superior record on the eastern tour.

Again, *Miss Madison* moved to the inside lane before the start and stayed there. The first corner was tight, with four of the five finalists closely bunched. *Miss M* exited the first turn in the lead with *Notre Dame*, *Pride of Pay 'n Pak* and *Atlas Van Lines* following in close pursuit and *Miss Timex* trailing. So evenly matched were the first four boats that they appeared as one long continuous roostertail down the first backstretch.

Miss Madison finished the initial lap one-fifth of a second ahead of *Pay 'n Pak* and two-fifths of a second ahead of *Notre Dame* with Billy Sterett Jr. As the boats went through the first turn of lap two, *Miss M* started to pull away, while *Pay 'n Pak* dueled with *Notre Dame*. The *Pak* moved away from Sterett on the second backstretch as *Notre Dame* lost power and slowed way down. Schumacher tried to challenge front-running McCormick but, in so doing, blew his engine and went dead in the water.

Meanwhile, *Atlas Van Lines* had gone past the ailing *Notre Dame* and then moved into second place. By this time, *Miss Madison* had an enormous lead and was putting added distance between itself and the *Atlas*. Jim McCormick was flat out-driving his more powerful and heavily financed rival. Now no longer considered an upset threat to win, the U-6 was making it all look easy.

At the checkered flag, *Miss Madison* had a full twenty-two-second lead over *Atlas Van Lines*. Then came *Notre Dame*, followed by *Miss Timex*, which was lapped by *Miss M* on the leader's last time around the course.

In winning the Atomic Cup, *Miss Madison* became the first Tri-Cities champion to do the honors with an Allison engine as opposed to a Rolls-Royce Merlin. *Miss M* also became the first Allison-powered craft since 1966 to score consecutive race victories in the Unlimited Class.

"This is really sweet," beamed a jubilant McCormick. "This should prove to some race fans that our Gold Cup win wasn't a fluke."

The *Miss Madison* team's triumph was now complete. "We're number one!" they proudly proclaimed. At long last, they stood at the very top of the racing world. In a sport dominated by millionaire owners and large corporate sponsorships, no one could afford to take the low budget U-6 for granted on the racecourse.

Following their back-to-back victories on the Ohio and Columbia Rivers, McCormick and *Miss M* competed in three more races. They blew an engine and didn't finish at Seattle but quickly regained their commendable form at Dexter, Oregon, where *Miss Madison* took a strong second place to *Pride of Pay 'n Pak*, the experimental craft that had finally gotten its act together. The *Pay 'n Pak* was not significantly faster on the straightaway than the other top Unlimited hydroplanes of post-1950 vintage. But with its low profile/wide afterplane design, the *Pak* could corner more efficiently than any previous boat in history. Handled by Billy Schumacher, *Pride of Pay 'n Pak* became the first to reach a speed of 121 miles per hour on a 3-mile course at the 1971 Seattle Seafair Regatta.

The boat of the future had arrived as the first in a new and faster generation of Thunderboats. The handwriting was on the wall. Inside of two years, every boat would have to be a *Pay 'n Pak* design to be competitive.

In the twinkling of an eye, *Miss Madison* was obsolete. The days of the box-shaped hull with the narrow transom and the shovel-nosed bow were gone forever. The craft that had debuted so many years earlier as *Nitrogen Too* had seen its better days. It was time to make way for the new generation of world-class race boats.

On the last day of its career, September 26, 1971, *Miss M* took an overall third in the Atlas Van Lines Trophy Race at Lake Dallas, Texas, with a victory in heat 2-A over Season High Point winner *Miss Budweiser*. The U-6 also tied down enough points to secure second place in the 1971 National Standings and thereby duplicate its 1964 accomplishment for overall performance during the season.

Miss Madison's year-end box score read 26 heats started, 24 finished, 6 in first place, 13 in second, 4 in third and 1 in fourth. This brought its all-time career total to an unprecedented 163 heats started, an even 150 finished, 26 in first place, 53 in second, 46 in third, 21 in fourth, 3 in fifth and 1 in sixth.

During the finale at Lake Dallas, the *Miss M's* deck started to work itself loose. McCormick kept it going at a safe conservative pace, finished the heat and brought the aging U-6 back to the dock for the last time.

A new *Miss Madison* represented the Ohio River town on the Unlimited tour, starting in 1972. Another *Miss M* carried on the tradition, beginning in 1978, followed by others in 1988 and 2007. And while each of these boats represented their thirteen thousand owners well, it is still the Gold Cup–winning hull that inspires awe.

In mid-season 1971, Jim started an Unlimited team of his own. He purchased the former *Parco's O-Ring Miss* (U-8) and ran it as *Miss Timex*—although he finished the season as driver of the *Miss Madison*, while Ron Larsen handled the U-8.

In 1972, he campaigned two boats—the *Miss Timex* (U-44) and the *Miss Timex II* (U-8)—and drove the U-44 himself. In 1973, he owned and drove two boats—the *Red Man* (U-8) and the *Red Man II* (U-81).

While attempting to qualify the U-81 at Miami in 1974, the boat hooked in a turn, and McCormick was thrown out. Jim suffered a serious leg injury, which left him with a lifelong limp. His relief driver, George "Skipp" Walther, was killed a few days later when the U-81 lost a rudder during a qualification run at Miami Marine Stadium.

McCormick returned to the driver's seat of the U-81 for the last two races of the 1974 season, taking a fifth at Madison and a fourth at Jacksonville, Florida.

In 1975, Jim briefly piloted Dave Heerensperger's *Pay 'n Pak* (U-1) but retired from racing after a third-place finish in the President's Cup. McCormick honored a previous commitment to campaign the U-81 (as *Owensboro's Own*)

Jim McCormick.

at his hometown Owensboro Regatta in 1975 but relinquished the cockpit to Howie Benns for that race.

Jim took one last sentimental journey as an Unlimited driver when he piloted the U-81, renamed *Santa Rita Homes*, at the 1977 Owensboro Regatta, where he finished eighth.

Between 1966 and 1977, Jim McCormick participated in a total of seventy Unlimited races and finished in the top three at nineteen of them.

Following his retirement from competition, McCormick suffered health problems and was for a time (in 1981) legally blind. Following laser surgery, which partially restored his eyesight, McCormick returned to the sport one more time in 1988 as co-owner with Bob Fendler of *Pocket Savers Plus*, driven by Steve David.

Years later, Jim was approached by a motion picture production company that wanted to do a theatrical film on his life and his victory in the 1971 Gold Cup. The movie, which was titled *Madison*, went before the cameras in 1999 with screen actor Jim Caviezel in the role of Jim McCormick. It was Jim's dream that this movie be made. Prior to his death in 1995, he had planned to portray his own father in an earlier version of the script.

When the credits roll at the end of *Madison*, a montage of outtakes from the ABC *Wide World of Sports* telecast can be seen. Through the magic of motion pictures, Jim McCormick was able to appear in "his" movie after all.

THE RON SNYDER STORY

Ron Snyder's boat racing career began in 1962. Competing primarily in the 280 Cubic Inch Limited Inboard Class, he owned and drove two boats of that description.

Ron raced Unlimited hydroplanes from 1974 to 1989. He is best known for his exploits aboard the *Miss Madison*, which he piloted off and on between 1976 and 1988. Snyder is the only *Miss Madison* pilot to drive three different versions of the world's only community-owned Unlimited hydroplane in competition. In 1976, he drove the Bill Cantrell–designed *Miss M*, built in 1972; he piloted the Ron Jones–designed *Miss Madison* (former 1973 *Pay 'n Pak*) between 1982 and 1988; and he was the first driver of the 1988 *Miss M*, also designed by Jones.

"I had qualified with Gene Benning's *Justa-Pest III* in 1974," Snyder recalls, "but it was the people of Madison who gave me the chance to prove what I could really do with an Unlimited."

The highlight of Ron's debut year with the *Miss Madison* was a third-place finish in the hometown Madison Regatta in the bicentennial year of 1976, behind Bill Muncey in *Atlas Van Lines* and Tom D'Eath in *Miss U.S.* It was obvious right from the start that this no-nonsense guy with the ready smile had "the right stuff." Indeed, much would be heard from Ron Snyder in the years ahead.

In 1977, as pilot of Benning's *Miss North Tool*, Ron scored points at every Unlimited race and finished third at Washington, D.C., Madison and Dayton, Ohio.

Hydroplane Racing in Small-Town Indiana

As driver of Bernie Little's *Miss Budweiser* in 1978, Snyder finished second to *Atlas Van Lines* in National High Points and won the Tri-Cities Columbia Cup at Kennewick, Washington. In the single most exciting duel of the year, at Madison, Ron and *Budweiser* beat Muncey's *Atlas* decisively in heat 2-A, after four dynamic side-by-side laps on the Ohio River.

Before returning to the *Miss Madison* team in 1982, Snyder guided the veteran *Miss Kentuckiana Paving* (former *My Gypsy*) to fourth place at the 1981 Thunder on the Ohio in Evansville, Indiana, for his old friends Cantrell and Graham Heath.

One of the most amazing feats in Unlimited hydroplane history was performed by Ron Snyder at Lake of the Ozarks, Missouri, in 1983. It had been twelve years since the *Miss Madison* had won a race. But Snyder took care of that in his own inimitable way.

The *Miss M* (disguised as *Miss Rich Plan*) made a shambles of oddsmakers' predictions. The top-rated *Atlas Van Lines* (with Chip Hanauer) and *Miss Budweiser* (with Jim Kropfeld) just plain "blew it" in the final heat. Hanauer and Kropfeld were so focused on each other that they weren't thinking about the rest of the field. When the starting gun fired, *Atlas* and *Bud* were way off the mark at the back of the pack, while Snyder—a past master of the clock start—was right where he was supposed to be, at the line, full throttle and going away.

Ron led from wire to wire and brought home the Missouri Governor's Cup for the city of Madison. Earle Hall and the *Squire Shop* took second place, and Todd Yarling finished third with *Miss Tosti Asti*, while Hanauer and Kropfeld embarrassed themselves, finishing fourth and fifth respectively, in one of the sloppiest performances of their distinguished careers. "I had won the Tri-Cities race with the *Budweiser* in '78," Snyder pointed out, "but that Lake of the Ozarks race—that was extra special."

Indeed, it was. Ron had won not because he had the biggest budget or the most up-to-date technology. Using a ten-year-old hull and an Allison engine, Snyder had defeated his Rolls-Royce-powered state-of-the-art rivals on driver ability alone.

Not all of Ron's races with the *Miss Madison* ended so triumphantly. At Evansville in 1986, *Miss M* hooked and threw him out during one of the heat races. Snyder suffered minor injuries. (While Ron recovered, Jerry Hopp and Andy Coker filled in for him.)

And at San Diego in 1988, Snyder and the *Miss Madison* were involved in one of the most incredible occurrences in motor sports. Ron was running head to head with John Prevost and *Miss Circus Circus* on Mission Bay. Both

Ron Snyder and Unlimited Hydroplane driver Fred Alter.

were chasing George Woods and the *Oh Boy! Oberto/Harvey Motorsports* entry down the backstretch on the first lap of the race. Snyder and Prevost then caught the same gust of wind and blew end over end. *Miss Circus Circus* broke in half and landed right side up; *Miss Madison* crashed upside-down. Never before—and never since—have two Unlimiteds blown over simultaneously.

Fortunately, both *Miss Madison* and *Miss Circus Circus* were equipped with the recently mandated F-16 safety canopy. Neither man was hurt. In Snyder's words, "If not for that canopy, I would have been shaking hands with the angels."

When Snyder started racing, he was one of the struggling unknowns on the challenging Midwest Limited Inboard circuit; when he retired, he had achieved the sport's big-time. He has a special place in his heart for the people of Madison, Indiana. "It was a wonderful experience driving their boat for them. I'd do it over again."

THE MIKE HANSON STORY

For ten years, between 1988 and 1998, Michael D. Hanson served as helmsman for the community-owned *Miss Madison* entry from southern Indiana. Following his retirement from competition, Mike's old friend Bob Hughes, president of Miss Madison, Inc., invited Hanson to return to the U-6 camp in 2004 as crew chief. The *Miss Madison* team, sponsored by Oh Boy! Oberto, has certainly benefited from Mike's participation.

While returning to the pits after one of the heats of the 1988 Seattle Seafair Regatta, the *Miss M* was run over by John Prevost and *Miss Circus Circus*. John had apparently gotten disoriented and drove right on top of the *Madison*, doing $50,000 damage. Fortunately, neither Prevost (who retired from racing shortly thereafter) nor Hanson was injured.

One of Mike's best seasons was 1993, when he and *Miss Madison* (sponsored by Kellogg's Frosted Flakes) finished second in National High Points and first in the Star Mart Cup on San Diego's Mission Bay. The 1993 San Diego race would prove to be Hanson's most unusual win.

The team was having a miserable day. Mechanical difficulties plagued Mike, who was unable to score points in any of the preliminary heats. *Miss Madison* advanced to the final heat on the basis of having finished first in the last-chance heat. This entitled Hanson to start from the "trailer boat" position, outside and well behind the other finalists. The trailer boat spot is the worst position on the racecourse. Never in the history of Unlimited racing had any boat won from the trailer boat position. But that's exactly what happened at San Diego in 1993.

Mike worked his way up through the field, through the battering wakes of the other boats. He passed one entry and then another…and another…and another. After five laps, *Miss Madison* was in the lead, taking the checkered flag. "I felt we had no chance to win," proclaimed a jubilant Hanson, "but I proved myself wrong."

Mike has three other victories as an Unlimited driver: the 1994 Texas Hydrofest at Lewisville with *Miss Budweiser*, the 2001 APBA Gold Cup at Detroit with *Tubby's Grilled Submarines* and the 2002 Bill Muncey Cup at San Diego with *Sun Harbor Mortgage*.

The stint with *Miss Budweiser* was a last-minute deal. While on leave from the temporarily inactive *Miss Madison*, Hanson was hired as relief driver of the *Bud*, following an injury accident to Chip Hanauer at Detroit. The *Miss Budweiser* team was battling to retain its National High Point Championship and needed every point that was available. Mike's performance in the "Beer Wagon" earned him the undying respect of Hanauer. According to Chip:

Even though he wasn't in the boat as much as I was during the season, Mike was just as responsible for winning the championship as I was. Because we needed every single one of those points that he earned.

We didn't know it at the time, but if he had finished second in even one of those four heats that he won at Lewisville, we wouldn't be National Champion.

Mike was in the worst possible set of circumstances—in a boat that he was unfamiliar with, and which was horribly damaged. He performed flawlessly.

Hanson's victory in the 2001 APBA Gold Cup at Detroit with the U-9 was one of history's most popular Gold Cup outcomes. That was the year when the winning Jones Racing Team lost their skid fin and suffered major structural damage the week before at Madison, Indiana. So extensive was the damage to the U-9 hull that the team's appearance at the Gold Cup seemed unlikely.

But instead of heading for home and missing the most important race of the year, Mike Hanson—a boat builder by profession—sparked a round-the-clock repair effort. For several days, Mike and his crew hardly slept at all. But when the starting gun fired at Detroit, the U-9 was ready to race. And what a race it was!

Sponsored locally by Tubby's Grilled Submarines, the Jones Racing Team posted a DNF, two firsts and a second in the preliminary action and earned a spot in the final heat. As the six finalists took to the water for the championship heat, the chances for a *Tubby's* victory appeared remote. *Miss Budweiser* (Turbine-5) had scored the most points in the preliminaries and had defeated *Tubby's* by five seconds in heat 4-A.

For the final, *Budweiser* had lane one; *Tubby's* was assigned lane two. As the field rounded the hairpin "Roostertail Turn" prior to the start, *Miss Budweiser*—the defending Gold Cup champion—encountered a roller and swapped ends. When the rest of the field thundered past the Gar Wood judges' stand and over the starting line, *Miss Bud* was sitting dead in the water with driver Dave Villwock frantically trying to restart. He did. But by then, pursuit was out of the question.

Hanson and *Tubby's Grilled Submarines* exited the first turn and pulled away to a decisive lead. The U-9, which few had expected to even be there after the problem at Madison, was on its way to the bank.

Tubby's averaged 140.022 for the 12½-mile distance. Greg Hopp, driving *Znetix*, took second at 137.605, ahead of Steve David in *Oh Boy! Oberto*, Mark Weber in *Miss DYC*, a fast-closing *Miss Budweiser* and Terry Troxell in *Znetix II*. It was "Mike Hanson Day" on the Detroit River!

Hanson had seriously considered retirement from racing after the 2000 season, following the death of his friend George Stratton at San Diego. But Mike decided to continue in the cockpit a while longer.

The 2002 Bill Muncey Cup that Hanson won at San Diego was destined to be something out of the ordinary. For the first time in many years, the turbine-powered Unlimited fleet was being seriously challenged by an Allison-powered "piston-packer." This was Ed Cooper's U-3 racing team from Evansville that was shaping up as a major factor after years of also-ran status.

Sponsored by Vacationville.com and driven by Mitch Evans, the U-3 led out of the first turn in the final heat with Mike Hanson and *Sun Harbor Mortgage* (U-9) in close pursuit, as the San Diego crowd went wild. Evans stayed ahead for two laps before Hanson finally overtook him. Nate Brown in *Miss E-Lam Plus* (U-16), running third, worked past the U-3 on lap four. And that's how they finished: Hanson, Brown and Evans, in that order. It was the kind of race that brings crowds back.

In 2003, his final year of competition, Hanson guided the U-9 to second place in National High Points. He finished second at Evansville with *Miss WABX*, third at Madison with *Miss Bello's Pizza* and third at Detroit with *Al Deeby Dodge*.

In 2005 and 2006, Mike was largely responsible for the *Miss M's* mechanical success. The team finished second both years in National High

Mike Hanson.

Points, and driver Steve David won the High Point Driver title both years. In 2007, Hanson co-designed (with Dale Van Wieringen and Ron Jones Jr.) a new state-of-the-art U-6 hull for the City of Madison. This craft went on to win the National High Point Championship three years running in 2008, 2009 and 2010.

Working alongside Mike is his brother, Larry Hanson, who is the *Miss Madison*'s turbine engine specialist. According to Bob Hughes, "I can't say enough for Mike and Larry. As a former driver, no one knows the inner workings of a race team better than Mike. He is the perfect communicator over the radio with the driver when a race is in progress."

THE STEVE DAVID STORY

A prominent Florida realtor who teaches college classes in real estate, Steve David is a lifelong boat racer. He has over 250 race victories in the Limited ranks and over 500 heat wins. A past president of the American Power Boat Association, David has served the sport well both on and off the racecourse.

His accomplishments in the Inboard category include four straight National Championship Race victories in the 1.5-Litre Stock Class with the Toyota-powered Constant Pressure between 1988 and 1991. He also won the Grand National Hydro Class National Championship Race with the Chevy-powered Steeler in 1990.

Steve made his Unlimited debut in 1988 with Jim McCormick's Pocket Savers Plus team and was named Rookie of the Year. His Unlimited career shifted into high gear in 1991, when he signed with the Harvey Motorsports team. The association was to last for nine years. Here was a pilot with tremendous driving ability and one who was also great in the publicity department.

According to owner Jim Harvey, "I've had other drivers who would complain to the press when they were upset about something that happened in a race. I had to ride herd on them constantly. But with Steve David, I never had that problem. I could walk away and go back to work on the boat, knowing that Steve would always represent the sponsor well and say what needed to be said to the media."

During the Steve David years, the Harvey Motorsports team never failed to finish in the top five in National High Points. The most satisfying campaign for David and Harvey had to be 1993, when they won the first and the last races of the season—at Lewisville, Texas, and Honolulu, Hawaii—with two different boats named *Miss T-Plus*.

Following a brief retirement from the sport, Steve David returned to active duty in 2001 as driver of the community-owned *Oh Boy! Oberto/Miss Madison* (U-6) from southern Indiana. This set the stage for a richly sentimental triumph in the 2001 Indiana Governor's Cup at Madison. Steve made a perfectly timed start in the final heat and went on to win all the marbles while holding off a persistent challenge from second-place Greg Hopp in *Znetix*. This marked the first victory on home waters by the U-6 team in thirty years. On the day following the win at Madison, the headline for the local newspaper consisted of two words: "Oh Boy!"

Miss Madison had long been a competitive presence in Unlimited hydroplane racing. But not until 2005 did a *Miss M* pilot succeed in winning the National High Point Driver Championship. Steve David achieved that distinction in addition to winning Thunder on the Ohio at Evansville, Indiana. David followed that up with a second High Point Driver title in 2006. But the boat was getting tired.

No one was happier than Steve with the announcement that a brand-new "Floating Chamber of Commerce" for the city of Madison would debut in 2007, thanks to a significant contribution by the sponsoring Oberto Sausage Company. In 2007, the new *Oh Boy! Oberto/Miss Madison* (U-6) finished an overall first or second at five of the six races on the American Boat Racing Association (now the H1 Unlimited) tour.

The first four races of the season belonged to the Seattle-based *Miss E-Lam Plus* (U-16) and driver Dave Villwock. The *E-Lam* team definitely had its act together. People began to wonder, "Is the U-16 going to sweep the season? Can anybody stop Villwock?"

It fell to *Oh Boy! Oberto* to snap *Miss E-Lam Plus*'s win streak. After having finished second to the U-16 in three straight races, the U-6 won the Chevrolet Cup at Seattle and the Bill Muncey Cup at San Diego. In both races, Steve David made a perfect start where it counted—in the final heat. *Oberto* led from wire to wire in the Seattle finale and held off a dynamic challenge from second-place *Hoss Mortgage Investors*. Rookie David Bryant made Steve David work for it every inch of the way. The outcome was in doubt right down to the checkered flag.

The finale at San Diego on Mission Bay was another classic. *Oberto* grabbed the inside lane before the start and forced the rest of the field to run a wider—and longer—track. Second-place Jeff Bernard, driver of

Formulaboats.com (U-5), went all out but couldn't catch the front-running U-6.

The 2008 campaign was the one that Madisonians had long awaited. The community-owned U-6 finally won the National High Point Team Championship. Steve David had won two Driver Championships. But the team had never finished higher than second in National Points. Steve wanted the Team Championship for the city and for Oberto. And he got it.

David started in twenty-one heats of competition in 2008, finished first in ten of them, was second eight times, third once, fourth twice, qualified fastest at four out of six races and won the Tri-Cities Columbia Cup. At season's end, the U-6 had 7,503 accumulated points, compared to 6,825 for second-place *Formulaboats.com* (U-5). This entitled the *Oh Boy! Oberto/Miss Madison* team to carry the coveted U-1 registration number, indicative of their status as defending National Champion.

Steve then proceeded to make it two Team Championships in a row for *Oh Boy! Oberto* and *Miss Madison* in 2009 with a total point accumulation of 7,970, compared to 7,735 for second-place *Miss E-Lam Plus*. David started in twenty-six heats of competition in 2009, finished first in eleven of them, was second nine times, third three times, sixth once and again won the Tri-Cities Columbia Cup. Steve flipped the boat in a preliminary heat at the season-concluding Oryx Cup in Doha, Qatar, but rebounded to finish second in the finale and claim the overall season title. David did this despite an as-yet-undiagnosed broken fibula cap in his right (throttle) leg.

The 2010 season was another triumph, with the team winning its third straight national crown and Steve winning his fifth High Point Driver title in six years. *Oh Boy! Oberto/Miss Madison* finished first at Madison, the Tri-Cities and Seattle, second at Detroit and San Diego and third at Doha. This marked the first time that a *Miss Madison* hydroplane had ever won three races in a given year.

The final heat at Seattle was incredibly suspenseful. Dave Villwock and *Spirit of Qatar* (U-96) stayed within Steve David's roostertail length the entire five laps. The outcome was in doubt down to the last two seconds of the race.

Steve started in twenty-six heats of competition in 2010, finished first in fifteen of them, was second seven times, third three times and fourth once.

In ten years with the *Oh Boy! Oberto/Miss Madison* team, David finished in the top three at thirty-eight races: nine of them in first place, sixteen in second and thirteen in third.

THE BOB HUGHES STORY

For four decades, Bob Hughes has been the guiding light behind the community-owned *Miss Madison*. As representative owner of the boat on behalf of the City of Madison, Indiana, Bob oversees all aspects of the *Oh Boy! Oberto/Miss Madison* racing program. He does this in cooperation with team members Charlie Grooms, Mike Hanson, Tony Steinhardt, John Humes, Hank Bentz and others.

It all started in 1965 when his friend—and fellow Madison businessman—Steinhardt asked Hughes for financial and machine shop support for the struggling *Miss Madison*. Bob not only obliged but, within five years, was serving as leader of the team's governing body. According to Steinhardt, who still serves on the board of directors, "That boat would have died a long time ago were it not for Bob Hughes."

Bob's contributions to the sport of Unlimited hydroplane racing have not gone unnoticed. Hughes won the Unlimited Sportsman of the Year Award in 1983 and the prestigious Gar Wood Award in 2003.

Miss Madison is the longest continuously active Unlimited team in history. The original *Miss M* was a gift to the City of Madison from industrialist Samuel F. DuPont and first entered competition in 1961. Over the years, a total of seven boats have raced as *Miss Madison*, although one of these was actually a rental.

One day that Bob will never forget is July 4, 1971, when the second *Miss Madison* (also acquired from DuPont) won the APBA Gold Cup on home waters in Madison, Indiana, with Jim McCormick driving: "I yelled so much I couldn't talk the next couple of days."

Hughes founded Clifty Engineering & Tool Company in 1961. Bob had past experience as a welder for an outfit called Williamson Heater. He later worked for Product Engineering Company (PECO) in Columbus, Indiana, as a tool and die designer. During his employment with PECO, Hughes dreamed of having his own tool and die business. After much planning, he was on his way, expanding from a small building about the size of a two-car garage to the present facility of enormous size, located at 2949 Clifty Drive in Madison.

Bob's beloved wife, Carol Hughes, was the *Miss Madison* team's most ardent supporter. She passed away in 1999. Carol was—and still is—sorely missed by the hydroplane racing community.

One of the smartest moves that Bob Hughes has made in reference to *Miss Madison* occurred in 2000, when he negotiated a sponsorship deal with the Oberto Sausage Company of Seattle. The initial pact was for the second half of the 2000 season at the West Coast race sites. Since 2001, the Oberto family has been the team's full-time corporate sponsor.

Hughes also deserves praise for his hiring in recent years of Mike Hanson as crew chief and Steve David as driver. Hanson occupied the driver's seat of *Miss M* from 1988 to 1998. Following Mike's retirement from competition, the position of crew chief was a logical next step for him. David had retired from Unlimited racing in 1999 but was persuaded to "unretire" in 2001. Steve has been an asset to the *Miss Madison* team and to the city of Madison, both on and off the racecourse.

In 2007, the *Oh Boy! Oberto/Miss Madison*, with Steve David driving, scored back-to-back victories in the Chevrolet Cup at Seattle and the Bill Muncey Cup at San Diego. Moreover, the team took second place honors at the Madison, Detroit and Tri-Cities races and finished runner-up in National High Points. This was a major accomplishment considering the boat was brand-new and the crew had to work around the clock to be ready in time for the start of the season.

According to Hughes, "None of this would have been possible without the support of our sponsor, the Oberto family of Seattle. If we had done nothing else in 2007, we wanted to win in Seattle. They have won other races. But this was their first hometown victory."

And in 2008, the U-6 tied down the first National High Point Championship in the team's forty-eight-year history. The boat took first place at the Tri-Cities Columbia Cup and finished first or second in eighteen out of twenty-one heats entered. This entitled the *Oh Boy! Oberto/Miss Madison* (U-6) to carry the coveted U-1 designation during the 2009 racing season.

Bob Hughes.

Two subsequent Team Championships were achieved in 2009 and 2010. Moreover, David piloted *Oh Boy! Oberto* to repeat wins at the Tri-Cities in 2009 and 2010 and also finished first at the 2010 Madison and Seattle races.

The 2010 campaign was especially significant for the team. This was the first time in fifty seasons that a *Miss Madison* hydroplane had scored three race victories in a given calendar year.

According to Bob:

> As a businessman, I recognize the importance of hiring people that are not only talented but who can also work with other talented people and get results. That describes the **Oh Boy! Oberto**/Miss Madison *crew.*
>
> I'm talking about people like Mike Hanson, Larry Hanson, Pat Furnish, Jimmy Gilbert, Cindy Shirley, Randy Gayle, Trevor Hanson, Matt Sontag, Richard Dunn, Bob Hudson, Travis Johnson, Steve Dean and others. They worked on the boat and gave driver Steve David a competitive piece of equipment.

According to Charlie Grooms, who works for Hughes at Clifty Engineering, Bob is "the glue that holds [the *Miss Madison* team] together. His managerial style is direct and firm. If you take a problem to him, he solves it right away and you move on."

THE GRAHAM HEATH STORY

The first crew chief of the community-owned *Miss Madison* was Graham Heath of Madison from 1961 to 1965. Graham was the one man in Madison at the time with the background and the wherewithal to put a viable Unlimited team on the circuit. It was during Heath's tenure that the *Miss Madison* hydroplane scored its first major race victory.

In the high-tech world of Unlimited racing, the owners and the drivers receive most of the attention. But without the crew chiefs, they would all be dead in the water. A crew chief is defined as an individual who regularly works on the boat and has charge of those who also work on the boat. Crew chiefs, over the years, have had varying degrees of authority, depending upon their relationship to their owner and driver, yet they are considered crew chiefs if they fit the above description.

Graham had to be more than just a mechanic. He needed the qualities of an engineer, foreman, father/confessor, arbitrator, bookkeeper, travel agent, truck driver, strategist and overall planner. It was Heath's responsibility to get the boat and equipment van from city to city—on time. It was his chore to see that the equipment rolled into town bright and sparkling, presenting the best possible image for the city of Madison. It was his duty to see that the boat was ready, from bow to stern. It was his responsibility to train a race crew so that it functioned at peak efficiency and in perfect harmony. Put succinctly, the buck stopped with Graham.

Heath had been a motor racing enthusiast all his life. From an early age, fast boats and fast cars had a special place in his heart. As a youngster, growing up on a farm about twelve miles north of Madison, Graham was fascinated by the exploits of such premier car racers as Gus Schrader, Emory Collins and Wilbur Shaw.

As a young man, Heath became involved in Model T Ford competition. He spent a lot of time hanging around local racetracks, where he met his lifelong friend Bill Cantrell, who was making quite a name for himself at that time as driver for the *Southern Star* racing team.

After returning from military service in World War II, Graham gravitated to the boats. He worked on and drove Neal Cahall's *Geronimo* on the Midwest Limited inboard circuit. During this time, Heath became acquainted with racing great Ron Musson. "He and I were great buddies," Graham recalled. When Musson started driving Unlimited hydroplanes in the late 1950s, Heath joined him as a crew member. At the 1959 Madison Regatta, Graham and Ron scored a victory in the Indiana Governor's Cup with Joe Mascari's *Hawaii Kai III*.

In 1960, Musson drove for the Samuel F. DuPont team, which campaigned a pair of fast boats, the *Nitrogen* and the *Nitrogen Too*. Heath helped out on *Nitrogen Too*, which won the Silver Cup at Detroit with Ron driving. By now, Graham was thoroughly enchanted by the mighty Unlimiteds, the Thunderboats of the racing world.

The bug bit him. More than anything else, he wanted to work on an Unlimited full time. And in 1961, he got his wish. DuPont had retired from the sport but had a special fondness for Madison, Indiana. He decided to make an outright gift of his older boat, *Nitrogen*, to the city. And a racing legend was born.

Nitrogen became the first *Miss Madison*. Marion Cooper was the driver, and Graham Heath was the crew chief. The *Miss Madison* organization in those days included the likes of Cahall, Dick Cox and Phil Cole Jr. Assisting on the day-to-day operation of the boat, Graham recalled, were "Bobby Humphrey, my right-hand man; Ben Schnabel, who did the hull work; Don Smith, Bob Neal, and Don Tuite."

Heath and company took fifth place in their first race with *Miss Madison* at the 1961 Detroit Memorial Regatta. Then, they headed west to participate in the World's Championship Seafair Regatta, where they won the second-division Seattle Trophy Race on Lake Washington. Graham remembered that race vividly.

All we had was one stock Allison engine, an old tool box, an old junk blower, one gasket, one fuel pump, and some odds and ends. I had maybe forty dollars in my pocket. As I look back on it, we had to have been fools.

We had all kinds of troubles that day. The exhaust pipe broke off, the fire was going down into the deck of the boat, and a bolt broke in the propeller strut. It seemed like everything was happening. But Bill Cantrell and the Gale V *crew, whose boat was out of the race, pitched in and helped and we won the first-place trophy. It was great.*

Unbelievably, the *Miss Madison* made it through the entire 1961 campaign with a single Allison engine and an all-volunteer crew. Like the rest of his co-workers, Graham had to work a regular job to make a living and raise a family. But he still achieved competitive results out on the racecourse—even without an equipment van full of extra engines and an acre of spare parts.

The first *Miss Madison* came to a sorry conclusion in trials for the Gold Cup at Detroit in 1963. The boat was completely destroyed, and new pilot Morlan Visel was seriously injured. In Heath's words, "All hell broke loose" as the *Miss Madison* approached the Whittier Hotel on the front straightaway of the three-mile course. "I don't think that I've ever seen water go so high."

Graham's good friends George McKernan and George Davis helped him recover the demolished craft from the watery depths of the Detroit River. The next day, while sifting through the wreckage, Heath discovered the cause of the accident. "A four-by-four with a bunch of pennants nailed to it had gone through that boat. I found it lodged in the left side. That was the end of the first *Miss Madison*."

Not to worry, the City of Madison was not about to lose its floating chamber of commerce for very long. The Ohio River townspeople had another hull, the *Nitrogen Too*, which had likewise been acquired from Sam DuPont. Losing the first boat and seeing Visel injured took an emotional toll on Graham. "Ordinary people would have given up," he admitted. "But not racing people. Racing people have got determination, adrenaline, and the drive. They come back. I don't know how to describe it."

So Heath set his sorrow aside and plunged into preparing the second *Miss Madison* for competition. The nationally ranked 7-Litre pilot George "Buddy" Byers occupied the driver's seat from 1963 to 1965. Graham had the highest respect for Buddy's cockpit prowess and considered him one of the all-time greats. "He drove and he drove hard. You could never tell what he was going to do. And he loved to psych the other drivers. The first time in the boat, he handled it like a veteran."

Byers and *Miss Madison* finished second to Musson and *Miss Bardahl* in the 1964 National High Point standings on the strength of being both fast and consistent. *Miss Madison* captured the 1965 Dixie Cup at Guntersville, Alabama, its first major victory. And Heath was honored by the Unlimited Racing Commission as the original winner of the Crew Chief of the Year award for 1965.

The 1960s were pinnacle years for Thunderboat racing. Even the necessary introduction of big-money sponsorship did not interfere with good old-fashioned sporting comradeship. "We had a good time in those days. Everybody helped everybody. They were good people, fun people. The work was hard. It wasn't easy work. But the people made it worthwhile."

Two of Graham's favorite people of that period were Jim and Yvonne Ranger of Detroit. At the 1965 season finale in San Diego, Heath was thrashing repairs to an engine the night before the race. While the *Miss Madison* team burned the midnight oil, the Rangers' limousine pulled into the pit area and provided coffee and sandwiches for an appreciative Graham and his bedraggled crew.

On race day, *Miss Madison* finished an overall second in the San Diego Cup with victories in two preliminary heats. And Heath had a couple of friends for life in Jim and Yvonne. For 1966, the Rangers hired Graham to start a new team from the ground up. The boat was the *My Gypsy*, one of the most popular Unlimited hydroplanes of its day. Heath, eager for a new challenge, jumped at the opportunity and made the most of it with the help of people like Bob Espland, Leo Mucutza and Hap Dexter.

The *My Gypsy* years, between 1966 and 1968, were happy ones for Graham. Under his direction, the team entered twenty-eight races and placed in the top three at thirteen of them. *My Gypsy* also took second, fourth and second in National High Points.

But there were down days. And the downest of days was June 19, 1966, at the President's Cup Regatta in Washington, D.C. The race that came to be known as "Black Sunday" claimed the lives of three top drivers in two separate accidents: Rex Manchester of *Notre Dame*, Don Wilson of *Miss Budweiser* and Heath's good friend Musson of *Miss Bardahl*. "I've been in racing where bad things occurred," Graham acknowledged. "But that was the worst blow to me that's ever happened."

Afterward, he did a lot of soul searching. "I thought to myself, 'We've got to be crazy. Sane people don't do this!' But there's just something about racing. It's in your blood."

That evening, Heath went to owner/driver Jim Ranger and asked, "Boss, do you still want to race?" Ranger said yes. And so they did.

At the next stop on the 1966 tour, in Detroit, Ranger, a rookie, drove like a champion and outran the veteran Fred Alter and *Miss Dixi Cola* in one heat of the Gold Cup. And later in the season, *My Gypsy* won the Seafair Trophy in Seattle. Graham recalled that day with particular pride: "That morning, Jim was nervous. He wasn't laughing or being his usual self. I told him to go out and talk to people and get his mind off things. But Jim was a racer that day. I was sure that he was going to blow the Allison engine. But he didn't. Then, at the trophy presentation, he started laughing. That was the first time that Jim had laughed all day."

Heading into the 1968 campaign, Heath received a phone call from Boss Ranger, who said, "I've got a boy out here [in California] who would like to drive the boat. He's a drag racer and his name is Tommy Fults." This was the start of what amounted to a father-and-son relationship between Graham Heath and the colorful Tommy "Tucker" Fults, one of the gutsiest—and most personable—men ever to jockey an Unlimited hydroplane.

Fults was lacking in experience around a closed course. So Graham arranged for "Wild Bill" Cantrell to give Tommy some driving lessons on the Detroit River. "The first day, Bill more or less led him around. It was the same the next day with Cantrell showing him the ropes. Then, on the third day, Tommy got the hang of it real fast and was outrunning Bill. He was doing some serious racing with Cantrell. Bill was a veteran and knew all the angles. And he taught those angles to Tommy."

Fults was a speedster and loved to go fast. But it sometimes took a stern taskmaster to keep Tommy in line. At the 1968 Madison Regatta, Heath gave Fults a monumental bawling out after Tommy fractured a rib during a misadventure with a motorcycle. Graham told Fults, "These people have spent a lot of money to get you where you're at. If you ever get on another motorcycle, your driving days for the *Gypsy* are over."

Tommy got the message, loud and clear, and toed the mark from then on. He went on to claim Rookie of the Year honors in the Unlimited Class with a victory in the San Diego Cup as his highlight. In that race, Heath counseled Fults to "not go out and chase Billy Schumacher and the *Miss Bardahl* in the final heat," this being in the days when races were scored by total points. "Just stay where you can see him. Don't let him lap you, but don't run with him." Tommy followed Graham's advice to the letter and won the cup.

After the retirement of Jim and Yvonne Ranger from racing, Heath moved home to Madison from Detroit. In the years that followed, Graham helped a number of Unlimited teams, including the *Miss Owensboro* and the

Mister Fabricator, and even sponsored Brian Keogh's boat as the *C&H Machine Special*, named after the shop that Heath and Cantrell had co-founded.

Between 1979 and 1983, Graham and Bill brought the former *My Gypsy* out a few times to fill out the field. "We were just going to have some fun with her. We didn't see ourselves as being competitive with the modern boats. But we ended up doing rather well. That's because we kept finishing and finishing."

Although obsolete, the old *Gypsy* was still one of the most reliable Unlimiteds of all time. Unfortunately, all good things must come to an end. For 1983, Heath and Cantrell built up some extra-powerful aux-stage Allison engines for their aging juggernaut. "We thought we had better get it pickleforked after what happened to Chuck Thompson at Detroit in 1966, when his boat flew to pieces. That was a big mistake. When Jon Staudacher put it together, it was nothing but styrofoam and wasn't fastened to anything. At 70 miles an hour, it came apart."

The end of the trail came at Detroit when the forward section of the hull disintegrated. Driver Jon Peddie fortunately suffered only minor injuries. But the last of the old-style Midwest riverboats was history.

Graham returned the shattered *My Gypsy* remains to Madison and then retired from racing. Heath recognized that turbine engines were the future of the sport. To change over to the new turbine technology would require an enormous outlay of cash. So Graham decided to call it a career.

But Heath wasn't ready for the old folks' home yet. "I started out in cars," he said with a gleam in his eye. "So, I went back to cars. I bought a midget, and I've been running it ever since…and having a good time."

Prior to his death in 2008, Graham still kept his hand in things Unlimited. He offered his expertise to the *Cooper's Express* team of Ed Cooper Sr. and Ed Cooper Jr. from Madison and Evansville, Indiana. And in 1999, Heath assisted in the production of the Hollywood motion picture *Madison*, which had a hydroplane theme. Graham was the one largely responsible for keeping those ancient Allison engines running for the racing scenes.

Appendix A
EARLY MADISON RACE WINNERS (PRE–INDIANA GOVERNOR'S CUP)

YEAR	WINNING BOAT	WINNING DRIVER
1914	*E.L.A.*	C.S. Gilbert
1915	*Vivo*	James Howard
1916	*Mohawk Kid*	R.B. Hadley
1929	*Catherine III*	L.J. Montifer
1930	*Miss Cincinnati*	Cam Fischer
1932	*Betty*	V.L. Bundschu
1934	*Big Shot*	Bill Cantrell
1935	*Big Shot*	Bill Cantrell
1936	*Why Worry*	Bill Cantrell
1949	*Hornet*	Marion Cooper
1950	*My Darling*	Andy Marcy

INDIANA GOVERNOR'S CUP CHAMPIONS (1951–2010)

Indiana Governor's Cup.

YEAR	WINNING BOAT	WINNING DRIVER
1951	*Hornet*	Marion Cooper
1952	*Wildcatter*	Burnett Bartley Jr.
1953	*Wildcatter*	Burnett Bartley Jr.
1954	*Gale IV*	Bill Cantrell
1955	*Tempo VII*	Danny Foster
1956	*Miss U.S. I*	Fred Alter
1957	*Hawaii Kai III*	Jack Regas
1958	*Miss U.S. I*	Don Wilson
1959	*Hawaii Kai III*	Ron Musson
1960	*Miss Thriftway*	Bill Muncey
1961	*Miss Century 21*	Bill Muncey
1962	*Miss Century 21*	Bill Muncey
1963	*Miss Exide*	Bill Brow
1964	*Tahoe Miss*	Chuck Thompson
1965	*Tahoe Miss*	Chuck Thompson
1966	*Tahoe Miss*	Mira Slovak
1967	*Miss Bardahl*	Billy Schumacher
1968	*Miss Bardahl*	Billy Schumacher
1969	*Myr's Special*	Dean Chenoweth
1970	*Miss Budweiser*	Dean Chenoweth
1971	*Miss Madison*	Jim McCormick
1972	*Atlas Van Lines*	Bill Muncey
1973	*Pay 'n Pak*	Mickey Remund
1974	*Pay 'n Pak*	George Henley
1975	*Pay 'n Pak*	George Henley
1976	*Atlas Van Lines*	Bill Muncey
1977	*Miss Budweiser*	Mickey Remund
1978	*Atlas Van Lines*	Bill Muncey
1979	*Atlas Van Lines*	Bill Muncey
1980	*Miss Budweiser*	Dean Chenoweth
1981	*Miss Budweiser*	Dean Chenoweth
1982	*Squire Shop*	Tom D'Eath
1983	*Miss Budweiser*	Jim Kropfeld
1984	*Atlas Van Lines*	Chip Hanauer
1985	*Miss 7-Eleven*	Steve Reynolds
1986	*Miller American*	Chip Hanauer
1987	*Miss Budweiser*	Jim Kropfeld
1988	*Mr. Pringles*	Scott Pierce
1989	*Miss Budweiser*	Jim Kropfeld

YEAR	WINNING BOAT	WINNING DRIVER
1990	*Miss Circus Circus*	Chip Hanauer
1991	*American Spirit*	Mark Evans
1992	*Miss Budweiser*	Chip Hanauer
1993	*Miss Budweiser*	Chip Hanauer
1994	*Miss Budweiser*	Chip Hanauer
1995	*Smokin' Joe's*	Mark Tate
1996	*Smokin' Joe's*	Mark Tate
1997	*Miss Budweiser*	Dave Villwock
1998	*Miss Budweiser*	Dave Villwock
1999	*Miss Pico*	Chip Hanauer
2000	*Miss Budweiser*	Dave Villwock
2001	*Oh Boy! Oberto/Miss Madison*	Steve David
2002	*Miss E-Lam Plus*	Nate Brown
2003	*Miss Budweiser*	Dave Villwock
2004	*Miss Budweiser*	Dave Villwock
2005	*Miss E-Lam Plus*	J.W. Myers
2006	*Miss E-Lam Plus*	Dave Villwock
2007	*Miss E-Lam Plus*	Dave Villwock
2008	*Formulaboats.com*	Jeff Bernard
2009	*Miss E-Lam Plus*	Dave Villwock
2010	*Oh Boy! Oberto/Miss Madison*	Steve David

Appendix C
MISS MADISON:
A FIFTY-YEAR TIMELINE
(1961–2010)

The community-owned *Miss Madison* from Madison, Indiana, is the oldest continuously active team in Unlimited hydroplane history. The city has had a boat in competition every year from 1961 to 2010—a total of fifty seasons. No other Unlimited team can claim such a distinguished record of longevity. By comparison, the late Bernie Little's *Miss Budweiser* team started in 1963 and retired after 2004.

In 2010, the *Oh Boy! Oberto/Miss Madison* (U-1) achieved its third straight National High Point Championship with Steve David driving. This entitles the *Miss M* to wear the coveted U-1 label again in 2011.

***

1961

In late 1960, industrialist Sam DuPont donated his *Nitrogen* hydroplane, an Allison-powered craft, to the City of Madison. The name was changed to *Miss Madison*, Graham Heath of Madison became the crew chief of an all-volunteer crew and Marion Cooper of Louisville, Kentucky, signed on as driver. The original *Miss M* took fifth place in its first race, the 1961 Detroit Memorial Regatta, and later in the season, won a secondary race at the Seattle Seafair Regatta in Seattle, Washington.

1962

A poverty budget and stock equipment not withstanding, *Miss Madison* did itself proud in its second season as the "Floating Chamber of Commerce" for the City of Madison. Pilot Cooper and crew chief Heath took fourth place in the Spirit of Detroit Trophy and third in the hometown Indiana Governor's Cup.

1963

The first *Miss Madison* ended its career where it began—at Detroit. During trials for the 1963 Gold Cup Regatta, *Miss M* was completely destroyed and pilot Morlan Visel was seriously injured. The former *Nitrogen Too* debuted as the second *Miss Madison* at the 1963 Madison Regatta and took fifth place with George "Buddy" Byers as driver.

1964

Miss Madison had a big year in 1964 and gave an extremely consistent performance. This allowed it to finish second in National High Points behind Ron Musson and the *Miss Bardahl*. Buddy Byers steered *Miss M* to second place in the Dixie Cup at Guntersville, Alabama, the Dakota Cup at New Town, North Dakota, and the President's Cup at Washington, D.C.

1965

After five years of trying, the *Miss Madison* team achieved its first major victory in 1965. Pilot Byers scored a come-from-behind win over Warner Gardner and *Mariner Too* in the Dixie Cup on Guntersville Lake. Another highlight of 1965 was second place in the San Diego Cup on Mission Bay.

1966

Jim McCormick of Owensboro, Kentucky, made his Unlimited Class debut as driver of the community-owned entry in 1966, replacing Buddy Byers. The *Miss Madison* team had a mediocre year at best. Their highest finishes were a third at the Tampa Suncoast Cup and a fourth at the Madison Regatta.

1967

Following a reduced schedule of races in 1967 with Ed O'Halloran of Detroit, Michigan, as driver, *Miss Madison* improved on its 1966 performance but was simply not the contender it had been under the helmsmanship of Buddy Byers. The highest finish in 1967 was second place in the Suncoast Cup on Tampa Bay.

1968

The 1968 season was a great year for boats like *Miss Bardahl, Miss Eagle Electric, Miss U.S., My Gypsy* and *Miss Budweiser*...but not for *Miss Madison*, which had one of its worst seasons ever. In four races entered, the boat was simply not a factor and failed to qualify for a single final heat.

1969

In 1969, the now experienced Jim McCormick returned to the *Miss Madison* cockpit. But even with the change in drivers, the boat's performance improved only slightly. A third at the hometown Madison Regatta was the team's highest finish. Indeed, the glory days of 1964–65 seemed light years away.

1970

A highway accident in Georgia while en route to the first race of the season in Tampa, Florida, delayed *Miss Madison*'s 1970 debut. Repaired and rebuilt by original builder Les Staudacher, the boat showed a definite increase in speed. At year's end, *Miss M* was running the best of its long career. It was ripe for a victory.

1971

Precious little can be said of the fabulous 1971 campaign that hasn't already been. *Miss Madison* and driver Jim McCormick continued the favorable trend that began in late 1970 with back-to-back wins in the Gold Cup at Madison and the Atomic Cup at the Tri-Cities, Washington. They finished second to *Miss Budweiser* in National High Points.

1972

A new boat (built by Gale Enterprises) and a new driver (Charlie Dunn) headlined the *Miss Madison* team in 1972. A championship season was anticipated. But this was not to be. Dunn crashed during qualification for the Gold Cup at Detroit. For the first time since 1961, there was no *Miss Madison* host boat at the Madison Regatta.

1973

Following the mid-season resignation of Charlie Dunn, Tom Sheehy became driver of *Miss Madison*. The team had, for the first time in its history, a commercial sponsor: Nestea Ice Tea. The boat's performance in competition was mediocre, with the highest finish being a fifth at the President's Cup in Washington, D.C., with Dunn in the cockpit.

1974

By 1974, it was pretty much conceded that the Ron Jones Sr.-designed *Pay 'n Pak* and *Miss Budweiser* hulls were the state-of-the-art in Unlimited racing. Still, *Miss Madison* would not be denied. With rookie driver Milner Irvin—a last-minute addition to the team—it was the best of the rest and finished a respectable third in National High Points.

1975

The *Miss Madison* team, frankly, did not improve on its 1974 performance in 1975. Occupying the cockpit this year was Jerry Bangs, a trial lawyer by profession and a hydroplane racer by avocation. In ten races as the U-6 pilot, Jerry nevertheless qualified for the all-important final heat six times and placed fifth in National High Points.

1976

Ron Snyder of Piqua, Ohio, became driver of *Miss Madison* in 1976 and placed third in the Indiana Governor's Cup. This led to his being named Rookie of the Year by the Unlimited Racing Commission. Ron is the only driver to pilot three different *Miss Madison* hulls in competition (between 1976 and 1988).

1977

Madisonian Jon Peddie became the first local resident to pilot the community-owned *Miss Madison*. A veteran auto racer and body shop owner, Jon piloted *Miss M* to fourth place in a field of twenty boats in the 1977 National High Point Standings and was honored as Unlimited Rookie of the Year.

1978

Miss Madison the fourth arrived in 1978. This was the former National Champion *Pay 'n Pak* of 1973, which had won so many races with Rolls-Royce Merlin power. Refitted with an Allison engine, the "new" *Miss M* finished second in the Gold Cup at Owensboro, Kentucky, with Jon Peddie driving and second in the Tri-Cities Columbia Cup with Milner Irvin.

1979

After a promising 1978, Madisonians were expecting a lot from their boat in 1979. The season, however, proved a disappointment. Mechanical difficulties defied the efforts of pilot Milner Irvin. Following a sixth-place finish at the Gold Cup in Madison, the U-6 team withdrew from competition to better prepare for 1980.

1980

The *Miss Madison* team rebounded with a solid 1980 season performance that effectively dimmed the memory of 1979. Milner Irvin steered *Miss M* to fourth place in a field of twenty-three boats in the National High Point Standings. With new sponsor *Dr. Toyota*, the U-6 finished third in the UIM World Championship Race on Seattle's Lake Washington.

1981

One of *Miss Madison*'s best seasons was the 1981 campaign. For the third time in its history, the team finished second in National High Points. At the season finale in Acapulco, Mexico, driver Milner Irvin risked his own life when he spun *Miss Madison* at high speed to avoid running over the fatally injured Bill Muncey, driver of *Atlas Van Lines*.

1982

With the retirement of Milner Irvin, Tom Sheehy, the 1973 *Miss Madison* driver, briefly returned to the U-6 cockpit in 1982 but was replaced at Detroit by 1976 driver Ron Snyder. Ron took runner-up honors at the Indiana Governor's Cup in Madison and third at the two Washington state races in the Tri-Cities and Seattle.

1983

By 1983, the old-style rear-cockpit/forward-engine hulls were pretty much obsolete. Cabover hulls were all the rage. But *Miss Madison*—the former 1973 *Pay 'n Pak*—still had one win left in it. Ron Snyder drove it to an upset victory over *Atlas Van Lines* and *Miss Budweiser* in the Missouri Governor's Cup at Lake of the Ozarks.

1984

The *Miss Madison* team picked up an important new sponsor in 1984, American Speedy Printing Centers. Unlike Rich Plan Food Service and Frank Kenny Toyota/Volvo in 1983, this one was for the entire season. Ron Snyder piloted the U-6 to second place at Syracuse and Houston and third place at Miami.

1985

Ron Snyder took a year off from driving for the *Miss Madison* team in 1985. He was replaced by Andy Coker, a veteran 5-Litre Class Inboard competitor. As the twelfth *Miss Madison* driver, Coker won Unlimited Rookie of the Year honors and finished second in the races at Miami and Syracuse.

1986

The 1986 campaign proved a mixed blessing for the *Miss Madison*, sponsored this year by Holset Engineering, which provided turbochargers for the Allison engines. The U-6 finished fourth in National High Points, but driver Ron Snyder was injured at the race in Evansville, Indiana. Jerry Hopp and Andy Coker filled in while Ron recuperated.

1987

In its last full season of competition as the fourth *Miss Madison*, the 1978 *Miss M* took third in 1987 National High Points with Ron Snyder driving. This included a third place in the Indiana Governor's Cup. At the last race of the season in Las Vegas, the name was changed to *Holset Mrs. Madison* in anticipation of a new boat in 1988.

1988

Three different boats raced as *Holset Mrs. Madison* (U-6) in 1988. The new Ron Jones Sr.–designed hull wasn't ready to start the season, so the 1978 hull was recalled from mothballs. The new hull debuted at the Tri-Cities but flipped at San Diego. The third boat was a rental, borrowed from the Ed Cooper team, to fulfill a sponsorship agreement.

1989

Mike Hanson, who had replaced Ron Snyder for one race as *Miss Madison* driver in 1988, became the full-time pilot of *Miss M* in 1989. Hanson would retain that position for ten years. He guided the U-6 to third place in 1989 National High Points and finished second behind *Miss Circus Circus* pilot Chip Hanauer in Driver Points.

1990

The 1990 season would be the last for the *Miss Madison* team with Allison power. Turbine engines were clearly the future of the sport. In its thirtieth and final year as a "piston-packer," the U-6 placed sixth in National High Points and finished second in the races at the Tri-Cities and Kansas City.

1991

Re-powered with a Lycoming jet turbine engine, *Miss Madison* became more competitive and was capable of heats in the 130-mile-an-hour—rather than the 120-mile-an-hour—speed range. Sponsored by Valvoline Motor Oil, the U-6 placed fifth in National High Points and finished second in the Indiana Governor's Cup.

1992

Miss Madison—like an oft-married woman—carried yet another name into competition in 1992: *Kellogg's Tony the Tiger*. This was a continuation of a sponsorship agreement that had its origin at a couple of West Coast races in 1991. Mike Hanson guided the breakfast cereal team to fourth place in National High Points.

1993

The Kellogg's-sponsored U-6 team won its first race in ten years in 1993—the Star Mart Cup at San Diego with Mike Hanson driving. Moreover, the *Miss Madison* scored more National High Points that year than any other boat but was officially second to the *Miss Budweiser* team, which used two different hulls during the season.

1994

Despite the success of 1993, the *Miss Madison* found itself without a sponsor at the outset of 1994 and had to miss the first few races of the season. Not wishing to see the demise of a thirty-three-year competitive tradition, Powerball Lottery stepped up to the plate and sponsored the U-6 for the Madison Regatta, where it placed fifth.

1995

Miss Madison had two major sponsors in 1995: Jasper Engines & Transmissions in the East and DeWalt Tools in the West. The boat blew over on the wind-swept Detroit River and suffered considerable damage. Driver Mike Hanson escaped serious injury. But, in subsequent races, *Miss M* wasn't quite the same and failed to finish in the top three.

1996

With DeWalt Tools signing up for a full-season sponsorship in 1996, the *Miss Madison* team improved considerably in comparison to 1995. With Mike Hanson driving, they finished fourth in National High Points and finished in the top three at four events. This included a second place at Kelowna, British Columbia.

1997

Miss Madison's perennial rival *Miss Budweiser* was really on a roll in 1997. Indeed, Bernie Little's "Beer Wagon" garnered most of the glory, as it quite often did in those days. *Miss M* nevertheless hung in there and made its presence felt. Mike Hanson qualified her for—and finished—the final heat at all nine of the races entered.

1998

Bad financial times returned for the *Miss Madison* in 1998. Following the departure of DeWalt Tools as team sponsor, operating funds were lacking. The team nevertheless entered the 1998 Madison Regatta. Mike Hanson, in his final appearance as *Miss Madison* driver, steered the craft to an overall third place in the Indiana Governor's Cup.

1999

Sponsorship was still lacking for the *Miss Madison* in 1999, but the team nevertheless made it to a few more races than in 1998. Hanover, Indiana resident Todd Yarling replaced Mike Hanson as U-6 pilot. Todd flipped the boat in a race at Barrie, Ontario, but rebounded to take third place at Norfolk, Virginia.

2000

Charley Wiggins, a promising rookie, started the 2000 season as *Miss Madison* driver but retired after a couple of injury accidents at Evansville and Detroit. Nate Brown finished the season. Under the sponsorship of Oh Boy! Oberto, Brown placed third, fourth and third at the Tri-Cities, Seattle and San Diego races.

2001

The big news of 2001 was the hiring by Bob Hughes, president of Miss Madison, Inc., of Steve David as driver for the Oh Boy! Oberto–sponsored U-6. Steve would go on to become the most victorious *Miss Madison* driver of them all. David's first win for the team was a triumph in the 2001 Indiana Governor's Cup.

2002

The 1988 vintage *Miss Madison*, now in its fifteenth season, was starting to show its age in 2002. In its second full season with the Oh Boy! Oberto sponsorship, the U-6 finished sixth in National High Points with Steve David driving. Highlights included a third in the Columbia Cup and a fourth in the Gold Cup.

2003

Oh Boy! Oberto/Miss Madison experienced mechanical difficulties throughout 2003. They did achieve a moral victory at Seattle. The *Miss Budweiser* team came to *Miss M*'s rescue when it suffered hull damage in a test run. Using the *Budweiser* shop, the *Oberto* crew worked feverishly to effect repairs and ended up taking third place in the Seattle race.

2004

Mike Hanson made a triumphant return to the *Miss Madison* team in 2004. Now retired as a driver, Mike made the transition to crew chief with ease. Nicknamed the "Boat Doctor," Hanson breathed new life into the aging U-6, which finished third in National High Points and took second place at both the Gold Cup and the Columbia Cup.

2005

Steve David scored his second victory as driver of the *Oh Boy! Oberto/Miss Madison* with a first place at Thunder on the Ohio in Evansville, Indiana. At season's end, *Miss M* was second in 2005 National High Points and David was first in Driver Points. This was the first national title in the forty-five-year history of the U-6 team.

2006

Oh Boy! Oberto/Miss Madison suffered hull damage at the first two races of the season at Evansville and Madison but rebounded to take second place at Valleyfield and Seattle and third place at Detroit, the Tri-Cities and San Diego. And Steve David was once again National High Point Driver. A new boat was now in the planning stages for 2007.

2007

The first new *Miss Madison* since 1988 made its debut in 2007, sponsored by Oh Boy! Oberto and co-designed by Dale VanWieringen, Ron Jones Jr. and Mike Hanson. An instant contender, the boat finished second in National High Points. Driver Steve David scored back-to-back victories in the Chevrolet Cup at Seattle and the Bill Muncey Cup at San Diego.

2008

After forty-eight years, it finally happened! *Miss Madison* was National High Point Champion in the Unlimited Class! It was also a first title for the sponsor Oh Boy! Oberto. Driver Steve David started in twenty-one heats of competition, finished first in ten of them, was second eight times, third once, fourth twice and won the Tri-Cities Columbia Cup.

2009

Miss Madison and sponsor Oh Boy! Oberto made it two National High Point Championships in a row in 2009. The team also won a second straight Tri-Cities Columbia Cup. Driver Steve David flipped the boat in a preliminary heat at the season-concluding Oryx Cup in Doha, Qatar, but rebounded to finish second in the finale and claim the overall season title.

2010

Oh Boy! Oberto/Miss Madison won its third straight national title in 2010. Pilot Steve David placed in the top three at all six races entered and was victorious in the hometown Madison Regatta, the Tri-Cities Columbia Cup and the Albert Lee Cup at Seattle. This was the first time that a *Miss Madison* hydroplane had ever won three races in a given season.

****

Over the years, other community-owned or sponsored boats have come and gone in Unlimited hydroplane racing. But none of those ever won a National Championship—let alone three championships. Only the *Miss Madison* team

Oh Boy! Oberto/ Miss Madison crew.

has demonstrated staying power. Their boats have aided many regattas by their participation over the past fifty years and helped to fill out many fields when racing needed boats in the pits. They are a credit to the sport and to the city of Madison, Indiana.

MISS MADISON RACING TEAM HULLS (1961–2010)

D uring the fifty-year history of the *Miss Madison* racing team, seven different hulls have served as the "Floating Chamber of Commerce" for the City of Madison, Indiana, on the Unlimited hydroplane circuit. However, one of these—*Miss Madison* (sixth)—was actually a rental, on account of *Miss Madison* (fifth) being damaged at a race in San Diego in 1988 and being unavailable for a race the following weekend in Las Vegas.

***Miss Madison* (first)**—1961–63

Miss Madison (**second**)—1963–71

Miss Madison (**third**)—1972–77

Miss Madison (**fourth**)—1978–88

Miss Madison (**fifth**)—1988–2006

Miss Madison (**sixth**)—1988

Miss Madison (seventh)—2007–10

All of the *Miss Madison* hulls have carried the APBA registration number U-6. *Miss Madison* (seventh) earned the right to carry the U-1 designation on the strength of winning the National High Point Championship in 2008, 2009 and 2010.

Miss Madison (first) was a gift to the city from industrialist Samuel F. DuPont. *Miss Madison* (second) was likewise acquired from Mr. DuPont. These two hulls had previously raced as *Nitrogen* and *Nitrogen Too*.

Miss Madison (third), *Miss Madison* (fifth) and *Miss Madison* (seventh) were built originally and specifically for the *Miss Madison* team.

Miss Madison (fourth) had previously raced as *Pay 'n Pak* and *Atlas Van Lines*.

Miss Madison (sixth) had previously raced as *Risley's* and *Seaco Aviation Fuels*.

To date, the *Miss Madison* team has won fourteen major races—three of these with *Miss Madison* (second), one with *Miss Madison* (fourth), three with *Miss Madison* (fifth) and seven with *Miss Madison* (seventh).

Over the years, the *Miss Madison* boats have occasionally used other names to reflect various sponsorship agreements. These alternate names include *Hamm's Bear*, *Miss Lynnwood*, *Barney Armstrong's Machine*, *Holset Miss Madison*, *Valvoline Miss Madison*, *Holset Miss Mazda*, *Dr. Toyota*, *Miss Rich Plan*, *American Speedy Printing*, *Kellogg's Tony the Tiger*, *Jasper Engines & Transmissions*, *DeWalt Tools* and *Oh Boy! Oberto*, among others.

MISS MADISON RACING TEAM VICTORIES

1. 1965, Dixie Cup
Guntersville, AL
Driver—Buddy Byers

2. 1971, APBA Gold Cup/Indiana Governor's Cup
Madison, IN
Driver—Jim McCormick

3. 1971, Atomic Cup
Tri-Cities, WA
Driver—Jim McCormick

4. 1983, Missouri Governor's Cup
Lake Ozark, MO
Driver—Ron Snyder

5. 1993, Star Mart Cup
San Diego, CA
Driver—Mike Hanson

6. 2001, Indiana Governor's Cup
Madison, IN
Driver—Steve David

7. 2005, Thunder on the Ohio
Evansville, IN
Driver—Steve David

8. 2007, Chevrolet Cup
Seattle, WA
Driver—Steve David

9. 2007, Bill Muncey Cup
San Diego, CA
Driver—Steve David

10. 2008, Columbia Cup
Tri-Cities, WA
Driver—Steve David

11. 2009, Columbia Cup
Tri-Cities, WA
Driver—Steve David

Steve David holding the
Unlimited Hydroplane National
Championship Trophy.

12. 2010, Indiana Governor's Cup
Madison, IN
Driver—Steve David

13. 2010, Columbia Cup
Tri-Cities, WA
Driver—Steve David

14. 2010, Albert Lee Cup
Seattle, WA
Driver—Steve David

OH BOY! OBERTO/ MISS MADISON: NATIONAL CHAMPIONSHIP SEASONS

2008

Evansville, IN
Thunder on the Ohio
Heat finishes: 4th, 1st, 2nd, 2nd
2nd place overall

Madison, IN
Indiana Governor's Cup
Heat finishes: 1st, 2nd, 2nd, 2nd
2nd place overall

Detroit, MI
APBA Gold Cup
Heat finishes: 2nd, 1st
"No Contest" on account of inclement weather

Tri-Cities, WA
Columbia Cup
Heat finishes: 1st, 1st, 3rd, 1st
1st place overall

Seattle, WA
Chevrolet Cup

Heat finishes: 1st, 1st, 2nd, 2nd
2nd place overall

San Diego, CA
Bill Muncey Cup
Heat finishes: 1st, 2nd, 2nd, 4th
4th place overall

****

RACE FINISH SUMMARY
1st place: 1 (Tri-Cities)
2nd place: 3 (Evansville, Madison and Seattle)
4th place: 1 (San Diego)

****

HEAT FINISH SUMMARY
Heats entered: 22
1st place: 9
2nd place: 10
3rd place: 1
4th place: 2

****

UNLIMITED NATIONAL HIGH POINTS/TEAMS
(1) U-6 *Oh Boy! Oberto/Miss Madison*: 7,503
(2) U-5 *Formulaboats.com*: 6,825
(3) U-37 *Miss Beacon Plumbing*: 6,681
(4) U-50 *Spirit of the Navy*: 4,194
(5) U-7 *Formulaboats.com II*: 4,039

****

UNLIMITED NATIONAL HIGH POINTS/DRIVERS
(1) Steve David (U-6): 7,503
(2) Jeff Bernard (U-5): 6,825
(3) Jean Theoret (U-37): 6,681
(4) Brian Perkins (U-50): 4,194
(5) David Bryant (U-10): 3,450

****

2009
Madison, IN
Indiana Governor's Cup
Heat finishes: 3rd, 2nd, 2nd, 3rd
3rd place overall

Detroit, MI
APBA Gold Cup
Heat finishes: 1st, 1st, 1st, 1st, 2nd
2nd place overall

Tri-Cities, WA
Columbia Cup
Heat finishes: 1st, 1st, 1st, 1st
1st place overall

Seattle, WA
Chevrolet Cup
Heat finishes: 2nd, 2nd, 1st, 6th
6th place overall

Evansville, IN
Thunder on the Ohio
Heat finishes: DSQ, 1st, 2nd, 3rd
3rd place overall

Doha, Qatar
Oryx Cup/UIM World Championship
Heat finishes: 2nd, 1st, 2nd, DSQ, 2nd
2nd place overall

****

RACE FINISH SUMMARY
1st place: 1 (Tri-Cities)
2nd place: 2 (Detroit and Doha)
3rd place: 2 (Madison and Evansville)
6th place: 1 (Seattle)

****

HEAT FINISH SUMMARY
Heats entered: 26
1st place: 11
2nd place: 9
3rd place: 3
6th place: 1
Disqualified: 2

****

UNLIMITED NATIONAL HIGH POINTS/TEAMS
(1) U-1 *Oh Boy! Oberto/Miss Madison*: 7,970
(2) U-16 *Miss E-Lam Plus*: 7,735
(3) U-5 *Formulaboats.com*: 7,564
(4) U-7 *Graham Trucking*: 6,689
(5) U-37 *Miss Peters & May*: 5,253

****

UNLIMITED NATIONAL HIGH POINTS/DRIVERS

(1) Steve David (U-1): 7,970
(2) Jeff Bernard (U-5): 7,564
(3) Dave Villwock (U-16): 7,471
(4) J. Michael Kelly (U-7): 6,689
(5) Greg Hopp (U-100): 4,251

****

2010

Madison, IN
Indiana Governor's Cup
Heat finishes: 1st, 3rd, 1st, 1st
1st place overall

Detroit, MI
APBA Gold Cup
Heat finishes: 1st, 2nd, 1st, 2nd, 2nd
2nd place overall

Tri-Cities, WA
Columbia Cup
Heat finishes: 1st, 4th, 1st, 1st
1st place overall

Seattle, WA
Albert Lee Cup
Heat finishes: 1st, 3rd, 1st, 1st
1st place overall

San Diego, CA
Air Guard Championship
Heat finishes: 2nd, 1st, 2nd, 2nd
2nd place overall

Appendix F

Doha, Qatar
Oryx Cup/UIM World Championship Race
Heat finishes: 1st, 1st, 2nd, 1st, 3rd
3rd place overall

****

Race Finish Summary
1st place: 3 (Madison, Tri-Cities and Seattle)
2nd place: 2 (Detroit and San Diego)
3rd place: 1 (Doha)

****

Heat Finish Summary
Heats entered: 26
Heats finished: 26
1st place: 15
2nd place: 7
3rd place: 3
4th place: 1

****

Unlimited National High Points/Team
(1) U-1 *Oh Boy! Oberto/Miss Madison*: 9,444
(2) U-96 *Spirit of Qatar*: 9,053
(3) U-7 *Graham Trucking*: 8,207
(4) U-5 *Formulaboats.com*: 5,574
(5) U-21 *Go Fast, Turn Left Racing*: 4,894

Above: *Oh Boy! Oberto/Miss Madison* National Championship team.

Below right: Martini Rossi National Championship Trophy.

****

UNLIMITED NATIONAL HIGH POINTS/ DRIVERS
(1) Steve David (U-1): 9,444
(2) Dave Villwock (U-96): 9,053
(3) J. Michael Kelly (U-7): 8,207
(4) Jeff Bernard (U-5): 5,574
(5) Brian Perkins (U-21): 4,894

Appendix G
OTHER HYDROPLANES

The following hydroplanes have a direct connection with Madison, Indiana. The hydroplanes have

- Called Madison their home;
- Been sponsored by businesses that reside in Madison and the immediate surrounding community;
- Been driven by one of the local hydroplane drivers; or
- Been owned by one of the local community individuals.

Miss Bello's Pizza.

Hinkles.

Miss Kentuckiana Paving.

Matrix/Madison Fudge Factory.

Miss Jean.

W.D. Racing.

Miss Tosti Asti.

ABOUT THE AUTHORS

Fred Farley has been a high school and college instructor and a writer for many years. Fred has written articles for numerous magazines, newspapers, program books and websites found on the Internet.

He has served as the designated "official historian" for the "big boats" (the Unlimited hydroplanes) of the American Power Boat Association since 1973. Fred provides data whenever needed by the news media and officials at the various race sites. He has attended over 250 Unlimited races.

Fred Farley.

Fred served as a consultant for the *Madison* movie, providing information to the filmmakers about the different hydroplanes and the 1971 Madison Gold Cup Regatta, which inspired the movie.

As a writer, a historian and a consultant, there is no one more qualified to write about the people and the events that constitute Unlimited hydroplane racing. Fred can provide more than just the "facts and figures." He can tell you about the people, who they really are.

The Madison Regatta is the fifth volume with a racing theme that Fred and co-author Ron Harsin have produced since 2003. According to Farley, "I basically write the text and provide some of the historic photos; Ron takes the contemporary photos, does the computer graphics and handles the business end. It's very much a 50-50 collaboration."

Originally from Seattle, Washington, Fred and his wife, Carol, moved to just outside the city limits of Madison, Indiana, where they have made their residence since 1999. According to Fred, "When I would travel the circuit, Madison was always my favorite race city."

In addition to his duties as APBA Unlimited historian, Fred Farley serves on the board of directors of Madison Regatta, Inc. (the race) and *Miss Madison, Inc.* (the boat).

Ron Harsin has a background as a computer consultant to companies like IBM, Motorola, General Motors, TRW, Eli Lilly, Procter & Gamble and Ameritech. The jobs have included a variety of tasks, including computer programming, technical writing, applications testing, systems administration, systems engineering design and project management. Ron also served as a college instructor teaching computer software courses.

Ron Harsin.

As a technical writer, Ron has several published technical documents and manuals created for the computer industry. The writing experience helped considerably with the written text, formatting and development of this book.

In addition, Ron is an accomplished BMI affiliated songwriter with several songs recorded by different artists, as well as an award-winning multi-time published photographer.

In the computer industry, Ron passed the exams and holds the following certifications: Project Management, Human Relations, Computer Professional, Applications Testing, Tech Writer, Microsoft Operating Systems, Microsoft Excel and Microsoft Word.

Ron currently owns and operates Precision Laser Graphics, a computer-based company that provides engineered CNC production work in addition to cutting and engraving services for business and personal applications. The company creates signs, awards, trophies, collectibles and unique gift items for personal use and for retail resellers. For business and industry, the company provides metal-based laser marking and barcoding and precision plastic/acrylics design cutting services.

Ron, his wife Ilene, daughter Jennifer and son Randy are lifelong residents of the Madison, Indiana community and spend each year caught up in the Madison Regatta activities.

Visit us at
www.historypress.net